The Roots of a Radical

JOHN A. T. ROBINSON

The Roots of a Radical

CROSSROAD · New York

1981
The Crossroad Publishing Company
18 East 41st Street, New York, NY 10017

Printed in the United States of America

Library of Congress Cataloging in Publication Data

Robinson, John Arthur Thomas, Bp., 1919-
The roots of a radical.

Bibliography: p. 164
Includes index.
1. Theology—Collected works—20th century.
2. Church of England—Collected works. I. Title.
BR85.R64 230′.3 80-26002
ISBN 0-8245-0028-8

CONTENTS

Acknowledgment

The lines from the poem 'Anonymous' by Sydney Carter, quoted on p. 87, are taken by permission from the volume *Love More or Less*, published by Galliard Ltd, © Sydney Carter 1970.

PREFACE

In 1960 I made a collection of pieces, which has since run to a third edition, garnering what I had written or spoken 'on the side' during the fifties, and I called it *On Being the Church in the World.* In 1970 I made a similar collection, *Christian Freedom in a Permissive Society*, representing the spin-off of the sixties. The fact that it was larger than the previous volume, and indeed than this one, reflects the pressure under which I was then working as a bishop. The lists which I have kept since I was an undergraduate record that I both read and wrote more during those ten years than at any other stage of my career – which to me is some answer to the excuse that busy bishops or ministers are far too preoccupied to read, let alone to write. Now in 1980 it seems an appropriate time to repeat the exercise for the seventies. Once again my main work has lain, as it did in the fifties, in the teaching of the New Testament at Cambridge, though in all three periods I have addressed myself in other books to the credibility of the Christian faith and life in today's world.

I begin with a survey of what the Spirit, as well as the *Zeitgeist*, may have been seeking to say to us, in the church and in the world, through these past two very different decades. But as no one could have predicted the sixties from the fifties, so no one, I guess, can simply project the eighties from the seventies. The ball could roll many ways.

The focal point of the book, and the connecting link between the pieces that follow, where there is inevitably some overlap with what I have written elsewhere, is to be found in the set of three lectures which gives its title. They represent a revision of the Selwyn Lectures delivered in 1979 at St John's College, Auckland, and other centres in New Zealand, and named after George Augustus Selwyn, the first, far-seeing bishop of New Zealand. Since the invitation came from an Anglican foundation (and I am most grateful for all the brotherly warmth I received), I used them to explore my own roots and to reflect on the organic connection, as I see it, between the richness of the Anglican ethos in which I have been nurtured and the fruits of radical thinking and action to which it has led me. For of course the word 'radical' simply comes from the Latin *radix*, a root.

More specific examples follow, in chapters III–VIII, of this link between roots and fruits, both in doctrine and in ethics. They take further the kind of concerns, both for sticking-points and for stretching-points, that featured in the previous two collections. All such exploration, whether in faith or praxis, represents for me but the implications of what it means to witness to the Word made flesh, the root from which any distinctively Christian fruit must grow.

What come between roots and fruits, namely, leaves and flowers, receive fairly short shrift in the biblical imagery. Leaves are what the barren fig-tree had to show, and Jesus did not stay to admire them. And the flower, for all its unsurpassed natural glory, is noted primarily for the fact that it fades. Yet in the last chapter of the Bible comes the statement, with its striking imagery, that 'the leaves of the tree are for the healing of the nations'. And *The Leaves of the Tree* was the title given to a series of pen-sketches by A. C. Benson, son and biographer of the Archbishop of Canterbury. They included, viewed fascinatingly through the eyes of a child, both B. F. Westcott and J. B. Lightfoot, who together with F. J. A. Hort and F. D. Maurice represent that Cambridge tradition of theology and churchmanship in which my own work has been most deeply rooted.

So I too have ventured to speak of a few of the leaves by whom I am conscious, often paradoxically, of being made more whole. For who would naturally include in that category a figure like Judas? Yet the process of what Jung called integrating 'the shadow' is perhaps the most critical one for growth towards maturity especially in the second half of life. And if those I have selected seem an odd lot they are no more mixed than the characters that Jesus attracted to himself and has continued to attract over the centuries. The fact that I have been sufficiently struck by them to turn aside to reflect upon them, in the first place in the spoken word, says something no doubt about me. But, more importantly, it says something about the many-sidedness of the gospel which speaks to the mystic and the atheist, the conservative and the critic, the rooted and the radical, mixed up so confusedly in each of us.

John Robinson

I

A TALE OF TWO DECADES

One of the things brought home to one by going round the world these days is not only how contracted space has become but still more how we now share a common time. In earlier decades this was not so. Setting foot for the first time in a country no more distant than Ireland I recall felt like going back a generation: they all seemed to remember my father and my grandfather as if it were yesterday! And in the past travellers have experienced enormous throw-backs – finding themselves seemingly in a time before the invention of the wheel. Yet today, as news flashes round the world in seconds and one can watch Wimbledon live by satellite in New Zealand, all that has changed. When on landing in Fiji I saw a Unisex Boutique, I knew *when* I was if not yet quite where I was. And the transistor radio, today's 'lord of the power of the air', has made us all children of the age, however remote our habitation. Pop songs are the same, the fashions, the cult-heroes, the economic climate, the political trends, even the spiritual 'vibes'.

This is effectively a revolution of the past two decades. And looking back, from wherever we are situated, we can see that each had a common 'feel' to a degree that has never quite been true before. There is a time for this and a time for that, said the Preacher (Eccles. 3.1–9), meaning, as the Good News Bible well brings out, that God 'sets the time' and we can but respect it. Yet now, as part of what has been called 'the humanizing of the *eschaton*' or end-time (for we have it within our own power to trigger off 'the hour of the ordeal that is to come upon the whole earth' (Rev. 3.10)), the *Zeitgeist* is global and determined increasingly by the spirit of man. And if we are to perceive what the Holy Spirit is saying to the churches and the world we must watch even more attentively the signs of the times, since they so largely betoken our condition.

In retrospect now we can see that the sixties were, the world over, a time for being out on the edges. They began with Kennedy and the 'new frontier', with 'freedom rides' and race marches. They ended with the students manning the barricades in Paris and man stepping out on the moon. It was a time for the cracking of containers, for the breaking out of the old 'establishments', a word, believe it or not, that we did not know in that sense till twenty years ago. It was invented by an English journalist, Henry Fairlie, in *The Spectator*, and I well remember first hearing it, as I walked down a street in Boston, and mentally noting it for the future. We may wonder how we got on without it. But we needed it only when we wanted to knock it. In Britain this was marked by the satires of the sixties, *That Was The Week That Was*, and all that. And it was epitomized in the unceremonious exit of that Gilbertian figure the Lord Chamberlain.

He still exists. In fact I had to write to him recently to decline the Buckingham Palace Garden Party, so doubtless he is usefully employed! But at that time you couldn't put on a play without his say so. He represented the paternalistic society – those who 'know best' what is good for us. But suddenly his empire was rolled away as if it had never been – and the walls did not fall. Overnight another phrase was born, 'the permissive society' – though the very name presupposed that there was still (in theory) someone to permit someone to do something. What it meant was that the controls had slipped – with all the follies and casualties that went with the multifarious new 'libs' (another word we did not know in abbreviation, except in 'ad lib').

It was the time too for radical Christianity. One has only to recall the phrases and titles which tumbled over each other: 'God is no more', 'religionless Christianity', 'Honest to God', 'The Secular Meaning of the Gospel', 'A Time for Christian Candour', 'the death of God', 'the New Morality', 'Situation Ethics', 'the New Reformation', 'the non-church'. It was the time in England of the journal *New Christian*, which gave hope to a lot of people. Indeed for many, as for Wordsworth at the French Revolution,

> Bliss was it in that dawn to be alive,
> But to be young was very heaven.

Yet by the end of the decade the momentum of what Bernard Levin brilliantly caught in his book on the sixties, *The Pendulum Years*, was largely spent. The 'way out' had gone about as far as they could, and there was nowhere else to go. I remember being in Berkeley, California (where else?) in the last throes of the protests as Governor Reagan and the rest were closing in, and it was a neurotic society, tearing itself and individuals apart. Since there was literally no further west to go, I vividly recall being told (in strict confidence) of two families independently who had their planes packed and ready to fly to New Zealand when the bombs started falling!

Then came the seventies, for America with the reign of Nixon and the silent majority, for the rest of us fortunately less extremely. As they were beginning I remember Harvey Cox, the American theologian and cultural weathervane, saying to me, 'The sixties were for tripping, the seventies are for centering.' That, I think, was a percipient remark. If the sixties were the decade for being out on the edges, the seventies have been marked, again to use characteristic titles, by a 'Return to the Centre', 'The Journey Inwards', 'Exploring Silence', 'Contemplating Now' and 'Roots'. There has been a turning inwards and backwards, a pulling in of the horns, epitomized by the withdrawal from Vietnam, the energy crisis and 'conservation' – another word I first recall hearing in this sense from the young of California (previously its image was confined to dusty preservation societies for ancient buildings). It has been a time for turning east and turning in, for the search for the self and the exploration of inner space, for the recovery of mysticism and meditation, integration and wholeness. But the other side of that coin has been a retreat from the social frontiers of the sixties, to a new conservatism and quest for security. The student world is a much quieter and duller place. When I was last through Harvard I was told that 80% of the undergraduates there were either pre-law or pre-med, which if one knows anything about America shows they have a pretty shrewd sense of which side their bread is buttered. And religiously the questions I find myself being asked as I go around are about the new fundamentalisms, the strength of the conservative churches, the charismatic revival, the fascination with exorcism and the occult, and the widely publicized attacks on the 'politicization' of the World Council of Churches. Ecumenically we appear to have become more rather than less turned in upon ourselves. Easter 1980, so far from heralding, as the hope was, a great leap forward in organic union, finds the churches becalmed and uncertain. Divisions too seem to be hardening between parties in the church. The going (or at any rate the shouting) is at the moment being made by those who would resist further erosion to faith or order, liturgy or morals, and in the Roman Catholic Church theologians are again having their wings clipped. Politically it is no accident that by the end of the decade Australia and New Zealand, Britain and, until a recent upset, Canada had all gone conservative. Symbolic of the seventies are what I call my 'three M's', Malcolm Muggeridge, Mary Whitehouse and Margaret Thatcher. Though I have nothing against any of them personally and indeed admire them for the courage of their convictions, I can never make up my mind which most represents all that my soul abhors!

Yet the seventies have been necessary. We had to have a return to source, a recovery of wholeness and the centre. And like the sixties they have been both good and bad, sound and sick.

So what of the eighties? There is bound, as always, to be a swing of the pendulum, and one can only pray that it is not going to be too violent and self-destructive as the reaction sets in to what, if present priorities in Britain are anything to go by, is certain to be an increasingly unequal and divided society, with tax-cuts for the rich and simply cuts for everyone else (except on missiles, prisons and police). Yet we should not forget that the electoral samples I took earlier were all from what we have learned in these years to call the white dominions. The rest of the world shows little sign of going that way, as Zimbabwe has since demonstrated, and we are in the gravest danger of being found on the wrong side, especially in the Middle East and Latin America, when the revolution comes or the oil runs out.

Economically too, wherever we are, the ring-fence looks bound to tighten. It bids to be a more illiberal, violent and hi-jacked world. With the taps and terminals in the hands of fewer and fewer in a growingly computerized society, yet with the proliferation of nuclear and other know-how out of international or even national control, the capacity of the determined or the desperate to hold the community to ransom promises to rise exponentially. The arms race shows few signs of being reversed, rather the contrary. And even if the 'plutonium society' could be guaranteed safe and healthy (which is about the last thing that can be said at the moment), the centralization and surveillance required for its maintenance must mean the erosion of many of the civil rights cherished by the humanist tradition. The freedom of the 'white liberal', with the luxury of relatively soft centres and open edges, appears increasingly nostalgic. But equally the *laager* mentality, of embattled centres and hard edges, of 'what we have we hold', is an invitation to spiritual, national and racial suicide.

Simply to return to the centre and there dig in is to have learned nothing from the past two decades. We must indeed have a concern for centres, but we must have an equally passionate concern for edges – and for neither at the expense of the other. William Sloane Coffin, then Chaplain of Yale and now Minister of the Riverside Church, New York, who was a typical figure of the sixties on trial with Dr Spock for opposing the Vietnam draft, wrote to me at the end of the decade as things were turning sour: 'Our slogan in future must be "Twice as radical, twice as non-violent".' I would suggest adapting that to form a motto for the eighties: '*Twice as rooted, twice as radical*'.

For a radical has to be a person of roots and deep roots, with the freedom and courage, as Jesus did, to go to source and speak from the centre. For this the centre must be strong, as it was for him, hidden in his relationship to God as *Abba*, Father. Without that, as Luther put it, 'we nothing can'. And over the years I find I have been driven back more and more upon the strength of the Christian centre. In fact some people think that I have become distressingly conservative in my old age! It may look like it with books like *Redating the New Testament*, in which I want to push back all the New Testament documents before AD 70, and *Can We Trust the New Testament?*, to which the answer is, if we know what we are trusting it for (which is not in any sense as a nautical almanac), Yes indeed. On the Fourth Gospel I am so square as to be almost indecent among my fellow academics. I actually do think that it may be, not necessarily *the* first Gospel, but *a* first Gospel, and written by John son of Zebedee! But then I always have been thus inclined. I remember being sent an off-print, at the height of the *Honest to God* furore, by a Southern Baptist from the United States who was using me and my writings on the Fourth Gospel as a stick with which to beat the liberals!

I believe in the centre, both biblically and doctrinally, because I am convinced there is every reason to do so *on critical and historical grounds*. But by the same token I am always open to follow the argument wherever it leads (even recently on the Shroud of Turin), and this makes me a frontiersman, alike in terms of theological freedom and of social responsibility. I have no wish to unsay anything that I said in *Honest to God* and I do not repent of any of the stands I took in the sixties, on Lady Chatterley or capital punishment, on immigration or censorship, on homosexuality or abortion, etc., etc.

Indeed, as I grow older, the more rather than the less radical I find myself becoming on most of the key political issues which are crucial for our survival. I could balance my three M's by my three P's: Peace, Power and Palestine. I have never been a pacifist – yet stopping rather than stepping up the arms race (let alone the madness, in its present state of bankruptcy, of renewing Britain's 'independent' nuclear deterrent) becomes a priority at almost any cost. We stare mesmerized into the abyss and hear talk of tossing in 'nukes' as though they were fire-crackers. I started much more 'balanced' also on the nuclear solution to the energy crisis, but become increasingly radicalized the more I study the alternatives and listen to the anodyne answers of its proponents. But to this I shall return in chapter VIII. Again I was fairly even-handed in my assessment of the Palestinian problem – until I saw it at first hand. As a student of Martin Buber (himself uncomfortably pro-Arab for Zionist tastes), almost all my initial contacts were from the Jewish side; my New Testament work leans me strongly towards the Jewish background not least of St John; and I hope there is not a streak of anti-semitism in me. Yet the justice of the Palestinian cause seems to me unanswerable and the Jewish response, especially in labelling as anti-semitic any criticism of Israeli policy, distressingly counter-productive. (For anyone prepared to have his eyes opened I would commend the lucid statement of the Dutch Dominican Lucas Grollenberg, *Palestine Comes First*, drawing on his long knowledge of the country and on Jewish as much as Arab sources.)

Yes, 'twice as rooted' – we have got to strengthen the centre, to be grounded in the Incarnation, which for me is the heart of anything distinctively Christian we have to say to the world or get stuck into in the world. But for the rest we must remain totally uncommitted, not constantly trembling for the superstructures of doctrine or morals or organization, or worrying about the dotted or dotty lines which divide us from other Christians and those of other religions or none. As I urged in my *Truth is Two-Eyed*, particularly there in relation to inter-faith dialogue, I want to see strong centres and soft edges, not soft centres and hard edges.

My hope is that after the street-scenes of the sixties and ego-trips of the seventies – from both of which I trust we can stand enriched – the centre still holds. I am persuaded that out of the turmoils we have been through, of belief and liturgy, of structure and ministry (and they are not over yet – especially in the matter of ordination for women or homosexuals or the divorced), the church may actually be stronger and freer and better placed, *if* it has the courage and hopefully the leadership, to launch out again into the deep. It has been chastened and reduced, but I believe that if we are ready to stand and face *both* towards the centre *and* towards the edges there is nothing to fear and much to hope.

Two symptoms, however small, may perhaps be prophetic. The first is the current interest in a figure like Thomas Merton, who saw the stripping-down of silence and contemplation (all, that is, that the seventies stood for at their best) as a necessary prerequisite of disciplined or revolutionary action. The second is the phenomenon represented by the American magazine *Sojourners*, which headily combines a right-wing evangelical theology with a genuinely other-worldly, in the sense of new-worldly, political radicalism.

Or one could restate the issue in terms of the perennial alternation and altercation through the different centuries and cultures of church history between two apparently equally biblical understandings of what is implied for the Christian by his 'citizenship of heaven'.

For the one side it means that the whole orientation of faith must be other-worldly in the sense of next-worldly. If, it is stressed, in this life only we have hoped in Christ, then we are of all men the most foolish (I Cor. 15.19). The earthly scene is but temporary preparation for the real life of heaven. 'There's another country I've heard of long ago' and 'Soul by soul and silently her shining bounds increase', as those who are saved from this wicked world find their true way home. So St Paul says, 'Set your minds on heavenly things and not on the things of earth' (Col. 3.2), and the Jesus of St John tells his disciples that he is departing out of this world to prepare a place for them (John 14.2). No one could deny that this is a strong New Testament strain and it has been re-emphasized of late to murmurs of ecclesiastical approval. And it *is* one side.

But equally, and apparently oppositely, is the strain which sees the Christian's citizenship of heaven as implying precisely the reverse direction – supplying not passports for heaven but passports from heaven. 'You are a colony of heaven', as Moffatt with a stroke of genius rendered the phrase in Phil. 3.20. Just as Philippi was set to be an outpost of the *pax Romana* and the instrument of another and higher civilization, so the Christian's colonizing commitment, so far from taking him out of this world, must drive him more deeply into it. Indeed later in St John Jesus is made to say specifically, 'I pray thee not to take them out of this world but [within it] to preserve them from the evil one' (John 17.15). And when he replies to Pilate, 'My kingdom is not of this world' (18.36), it is clear from the Greek that he means that it is not '*from*' this world

– it does not find its source or resources in it – not that it is not for it. The central clause of the Lord's Prayer is 'thy kingdom come – on earth as in heaven', and the Bible ends with the vision not of heaven as opposed to earth but of a new heaven and a new earth, which is to be, as the Second Epistle of Peter puts it, which can most explicitly be quoted for the spiritualizing ideal of 'divinization' (1.4), 'the home of justice' (3.13).

So the pendulum swings between the two positions, held with equal sincerity and conviction, of those who think politics a distraction from the true priorities of the biblical Christian and of those who find them a demand which will never let them rest.

Clearly there cannot be an either-or here, and something has gone wrong if we suppose there is. In fact the most creative thinking in the church arises precisely when the two emphases are held most strongly *together*. The radical other-worldliness of the apostolic witness, 'We must obey God rather than man', leads constantly to prophetic stands for justice and freedom, as the Trevor Huddlestons and Daniel Berrigans, the Martin Luther Kings and Desmond Tutus of this generation have shown. The days when Billy Graham could be quoted as saying, in relation to Watergate, 'I am a New Testament evangelist, not an Old Testament prophet' are, one trusts, passing (as a recent interview in *Sojourners* on nuclear weapons would indicate) – for that is a most unbiblical antithesis. If the combination represented by this journal or in a different idiom by Thomas Merton could really take on, then I could see an explosive church witness for the eighties. But I fear the sterile sniping, say, of Edward Norman's Reith Lectures on *Christianity and World Order* appeals more to the mood of the rank and file, and the signs of a *Sojourners* theology sweeping the conservative evangelicals of the Church of England (certainly as I observe them in Cambridge) are about as small as the letters of John Stott's name as British 'Contributing Editor'.

Yet we live as Christians by hope and not by optimism, and the longer I go on the more I want to distinguish the two – the latter being based on rosy prospects, which for the eighties are not in strong supply, the former, as St Paul says, on the endurance born of suffering. And it is in the worst times that much of the church's best theology has been done. As St Augustine recognized as his world fell apart, the choice is not between the concerns of heaven and the concerns of earth nor between the things of God and the things of Caesar (it was Hitler who thought these could be alternatives). It is between two very different foundations for the whole of living. In the well-known words of *The City of God*, 'two loves have created two cities' – the earthly city grounded in 'love of self to the contempt of God', the heavenly on 'love of God to the contempt of self'. And the Christian's mission in this world, the citizenship committed to him by his baptism, is to transform the one into the other. In the words of the Epistle to the Hebrews (11.16), it is to 'seek a better country, that is, a heavenly one' – yet not by going out of this world but by bringing heaven down into it.

Two quotations could sum up the double concern for which I am pleading. The first is from the hymn by W. Russell Bowie, inspired by St John the Divine's vision of the new Jerusalem:

> Already in the mind of God
>   that city riseth fair:
> Lo, how its splendour challenges
>   the souls that greatly dare:
> Yea, bids us seize the whole of life
>   and build its glory there.

The other is from the Australian, Patrick White, who places at the front of his novel *The Solid Mandala* the words of Paul Eluard:

> There is another world, but it is in this one.

Such is the inseparable unity between centres and edges, roots and fruits, to which the spiritual combat, however from decade to decade the lines may sway, continually calls us back and calls us on.

II

THE ROOTS OF A RADICAL

1. A LARGE ROOM

I was born and bred under the shadow of Canterbury Cathedral – my father and my mother's father were Canons there – and if you are an Anglican you can't get much nearer than that to the heart of the establishment. St Paul speaks to Gentile Christians of the 'root and sap' of the olive into which they have been grafted (Rom. 11.17). And it is to that root and sap of my own Anglican ethos that I want to come back. I say 'come back', because I have been of late far from home. On an earlier trip, which led to my book *Truth is Two-Eyed*, my wife and I went round the world keeping on travelling east. We went, deliberately, to be stretched, to force ourselves to look at truth through the unfamiliar vision of India and the East. This is very necessary if one is not to grow one-eyed, blinkered and complacent. Yet, as Eliot said, the end of all our exploring is to return and know the place for the first time. So now I am doing the journey the other way round – to come home. Indeed, despite being in New Zealand at the greatest geographical distance from England, I feel I am *Never Far from Home* – the title chosen for his delightful and moving autobiography by the American New Testament scholar, John Knox, as dear and fruitful a branch to be grafted into the stock of the Anglican olive as any it has been my privilege to know.

I too want to speak out of the richness of my store. Have no fear; I am not writing an autobiography. That, if it ever comes, must wait till the fruit is ripe and ready to fall. Yet I shall not be speaking in the abstract about Anglicanism, presuming to define its essence or pronounce on its future. I am not out to prove anything. I am not saying that this is what it should be, or this is how everybody, or anybody, else ought to see it. It is much more reflections on 'my kind of Anglicanism'.

But to put it like that would be to falsify from the start. It would be both too individualistic and too modern a way of putting it. For Anglicanism is not 'mine'. 'Remember', says St Paul, 'it is not you who sustain the root: the root sustains you' (Rom. 11.18). It is much more like what the Old Testament characters meant when they spoke of 'I and my fathers'. They are referring to their patrimony, their inheritance, their 'land' (a concept as much spiritual as geographical). It is the patriarchal 'we' (very different in tone from the papal 'we' or the royal 'we'), which enabled the Israelite to speak of 'our' soul – the experienced reality behind that elusive idea referred to by scholars as the 'corporate personality'. The soul flows in and out between individuals and generations: the 'I' has no strictly patrolled boundaries or frontier-fences. As in primitive religions, the soul, like the collective unconscious, wanders across the tribe and across the centuries: it is not confined to the individual. 'The faith of our fathers' is not the faith that they used to have (like 'my grandmother's religion' – George McLeod once disrespectfully described Bultmann's demythologizing exercise as 'knocking my grandmother's religion with my grandfather's science'): it is the faith that I have in their continuing company, however far the caravan may have moved on.

That phrase 'the faith of our fathers' is the title of a most attractive book about perhaps the most attractive period of Anglican history. It is a description by Florence Higham, a member of the congregation of Southwark Cathedral when I was a bishop there, of the 'men and movements of the seventeenth century', and though I am not a historian this is where instinctively I feel my soul is most 'at home'. Which brings me to the other infelicity of 'my sort of Anglicanism'. For at that period the word 'Anglicanism' had still not been invented. Like most 'isms' it was a nineteenth-century creation. It is first quoted by the latest supplement to the *Oxford English Dictionary* from Newman in 1838. And, like most 'isms', distrust it. For an 'ism' is making a 'thing', a whole, an idol, of a part. And somewhere lurking behind it you can catch the abstraction of the German '*ismus*'.

It is an interesting lexicographical fact that most words ending in 'ism' are later than the corresponding word ending in 'ist'. For instance, humanism is a nineteenth-century creation – making a

Weltanschauung (a German monster again) or whole way of life out of a vital but partial insight. The humanists were much earlier – and they thought of themselves as Christian humanists, as opposed to humanism which is an alternative self-sufficient world-view. A giant among them was a man like Erasmus – a Dutchman, to be sure, but thanks to his Cambridge exile an *anima naturaliter Anglicana*! And I have always had a special fellow-feeling for him since I discovered that his *In Praise of Folly* was, like my *Honest to God*, the product of a slipped disc!

Or take the words 'scientism' and 'scientist' – though here the process is much more recent. 'Scientism' is a twentieth-century horror describing the notion that the whole richness of the world can be reduced and confined to explanation in scientific categories – a view that only the small-minded could ever conceive. Yet 'scientist' is of course much older – though I wonder how many could guess how much, or rather how little, older. For the word 'scientist' was invented, believe it or not, by William Whewell, Master of Trinity College, Cambridge, in 1840! And he invented, to boot, the modern use of the term 'physicist', not to mention giving names to such beasts as 'anode' and 'cathode' at the request of Faraday. One wonders how they got on without it, but of course they talked, as still in the names of the older scientific chairs, of 'natural philosophy'.

Or take another 'ism' which people suppose is as old as the hills – 'fundamentalism'. Would you believe that it is not in the *Oxford English Dictionary*? I didn't. But it is so recent that it is only in the Supplement. Its first recorded use in England is in the *Daily Mail* of 1923 – although it was born in America a few years earlier and is just about as old as I am! To make an 'ism' out of an uncritical use of scripture (which of course is as hoary as anything) is a very modern and I think a very nasty thing.

I confess my greatest disillusionment in this 'ism' game came with the word 'Quakerism'. When I first heard it I said, 'No, it cannot be'. For the great thing, I thought, about the Quakers was precisely that they had resisted this process. Unlike the Methodists, here was one society that had refused to become a church; they have remained what they call themselves, a Society of Friends. But, alas, 'Quakerism' goes back to the seventeenth century. It is first quoted from 1656, only three years later than the first recorded use of 'Quaker'. But 'Presbyterianism', I discover, is the oldest of them all, from 1644, again only three years after the first occurrence of 'Presbyterian' – whereas 'Anglican' is first recorded in 1635 *more than two centuries* before it got turned into a system. I should like to think that that corresponds to a real difference.

The other thing about 'Anglicanism' is that it designates it as a 'denomination' (another nineteenth-century usage in this sense) defining it after a name – though, thank goodness, we never got called Hookerites, even by our worst enemies, as others got called Lutherans or Calvinists or even Wesleyans. And how Wesley's soul would have abhorred that! For John Wesley, whose boast was that he lived and died a priest of the Church of England, was in many ways 'the complete Church of England man', a title to which I remember speaking years ago as my ideal in the Wesley Memorial Church in Cambridge. And this ideal is the very opposite of anything denominational or sectarian. In fact I recall an Australian Presbyterian contemporary of mine at Cambridge saying, and how right he was, that the Anglican church is not very good at being a sect. If you want contemporary proof of that, look at the continuing Anglican Church of North America, where the splinter has already splintered and indeed changed its name: ACNE evidently sounded too much like a disease! In fact as an 'ism' 'Episcopalianism' is an even greater horror, making an 'ism' out of the mere fact of having bishops. This Presbyterian friend of mine was also unenthusiastic about Methodism as a separate denomination, since to him Methodists were simply methodical Anglicans – and would that they had been allowed to remain so.

For the Anglican ethos is essentially catholic rather than sectarian. Its ideal from the beginning was a comprehensive settlement, though it tried to enforce that, in the mode of the day, by an Act of Uniformity – and has there ever been any church less uniform? But even when the ideal broke down, it never completely broke up. The parochial system kept alive the presumption that every man, woman and child formed part of the 'cure' of the pastor, and the practice of occasional conformity was at its best more than a political device for retaining office. The parish church was the church of the parish – even for those who were ejected from it. Florence Higham's *Faith of our Fathers* covers 'men and movements of the seventeenth century' not just Anglicans. And what a company they were! Not simply the Church of England men, Richard Hooker and Launcelot Andrewes, John Donne and George Herbert, Nicholas Ferrar and Thomas Ken, Jeremy Taylor and Benjamin Wychcote the Cambridge Platonist, not to mention the, to me, less attractive figure of William Laud with his very unAnglican policy of 'thorough' (though who was more thorough in the best sense than

Bishop Selwyn?), but my own namesake John Robinson, Richard Baxter, John Bunyan and George Fox. These were what Baxter in his lovely hymn 'He wants not friends that hath thy love' (which I would hope to have at my funeral as we had Charles Wesley's 'O thou who camest from above' for our wedding) called 'the several vessels of thy fleet'. And I still remember the text I was sent for my ordination by Roy Whitehorn, then Principal of Westminster, the Presbyterian College at Cambridge, on whose books I have the honour to be the only Anglican bishop: 'They signalled to their partners in the other boat.' That is how at their best (though, alas, not always) Anglicans have regarded their fellow-churchmen beyond the bounds of the Anglican Communion – and indeed within it.

For this brings me to my main point – that Anglicans have always regarded *themselves* as partners in a fishing fleet, or, to change the metaphor, as a flock rather than a fold. And in this corporate enterprise there has been room for much diversity and even divergence. I have always liked the title of David Newsome's book on the men and movements of another attractive Anglican period, early nineteenth-century evangelicalism, *The Parting of Friends*. The pain is still within the family; and it is from the family, my own family, that I should like if I may to start, in order to sketch, as in a microcosm, the breadth of the Anglican 'soul'. If Alex Haley can write about his *Roots* I don't see why I can't about mine (though at *much* more modest length!). Indeed a friend has suggested that there should be a book under the title *An English Family Robinson*! So I propose to recite something of what the Maoris would call my *whakapapa*, my genealogy, to invoke the presence and power of my ancestors, whose faith is my faith.

My father died when I was nine, having been born as long ago at 1856, three years before Darwin's *Origin of Species*, which makes him really antediluvian! So there was a big generation-gap, bridged by the memories of my mother, who, although we kept the centenary of her birth in 1979, died less than five years ago. There were two texts from the Psalms which she used to pass on to us as favourites of my father's, one from 16.6, 'The lot is fallen unto me in a fair ground, yea, I have a goodly heritage', and the other from 31.8, 'Thou . . . has set my feet in a large room.' If you will bear with me briefly, I should like to sketch in something of that heritage. For not only is it vital to my roots – it is *for me* the sap and richness of the olive – but it illustrates better than any impersonal statements could the 'large room' of which I would speak, the spread and the spirit of the Anglican ethos. If at times I may appear to boast it is, with St Paul, in the things that reveal the weakness and poverty of this generation (if only in classical learning). And nowhere is it clearer that the root sustains me rather than the other way round.

The roots of my father's generation go back to Irish evangelicalism of the mid-nineteenth century. And that *was* evangelicalism! I still have my grandfather's notebooks, with the contemporary tracts, of the great Belfast revival of 1859 for which he specially returned. The fervour and the piety could not be matched today even in the most charismatic circles. Yet my grandfather had left his beloved mission-work in Ireland because even at that time he could not feel that it was a prime duty of a minister of the gospel to spend his time knocking the Roman Catholics. He applied and was chosen, amid strong competition in those days, for a vacant curacy at Clapham parish church, the home earlier of William Wilberforce and the Clapham sect, whose vicar was then a Mr Bradley, the father both of the Oxford philosopher and of a subsequent Dean of Westminster whom my uncle was in due course to succeed. A few years later my grandfather was offered the vicarage of Keynsham, a village between Bristol and Bath. Here amid ardent work were born twelve of his thirteen children, the last following when he moved to a poor parish at Everton in Liverpool, partly so that his sons might get the training to go into business. But it was not to be. Of the eight sons, six were ordained (two being pioneer missionaries in Africa) and the other two became a missionary doctor and a missionary schoolmaster, also in Africa. Of the five daughters, one married a parson, two were deaconesses, one was among the first women to read theology at Oxford, and one, described as being 'of a singularly gentle nature' and whose letters reveal a 'naturally Christian soul' evidently somewhat suspect to the more pious of them, died of consumption in Sydney at the age of 21, where I spent some time tracking down her grave. Indeed no less than four of the children got as far as Australia, no mean feat in those days, and my father got to New Zealand as well, remaining Commissary for the Diocese of Christchurch for many years afterwards. Not for nothing was the family motto instilled into us: *non nobis solum sed toti mundo nati*, 'Not for ourselves alone but for the whole world are we born.'

But it is the range of their spirituality that here interests me most. They all began from the deep and unforced, if to us oppressive, piety of this evangelical home. Indeed the influence of the old mother, who far outlived my grandfather to the age of 92, dying only when I myself was on the way, was pervasive to the end. I savour the way in which Edward, the only one actually to react as a student, incredible as it now seems, *against* their religious upbringing, later described the naturalness of her religious conversation:

> One would think of some people if they talked as Mother did that they'd settled themselves in to be serious. But no – with her it was as if one referred for a few moments to a favourite hobby, never in danger of being neglected, and therefore not to be nervously insisted upon.

And from this seed-bed was to come to slow maturity an astonishing luxuriance of spiritual and intellectual growth. I must be drastically selective.

The most famous of them was Armitage, who had a brilliant academic career at Cambridge, growing up, as they all did, under 'the cedar tree' of Lightfoot (to whom he was later domestic chaplain), Westcott and Hort. In fact that whole generation regarded themselves as a race of dwarfs, but what giants they now seem. Armitage was thought destined by many to be the English Harnack, and he had a knowledge of early Christian literature in the original languages unrivalled in the English-speaking world. But again it was not to be. After his commentary on the Epistle to the Ephesians, still perhaps the greatest in the field, he dissipated his learning (so many would say) as Dean of Westminster and subsequently of Wells in ecclesiastical antiquities. But it is the spread of his large mind which is so fascinating. As a young fellow of Christ's College he was the first to teach the New Testament at Ridley Hall, the newly founded evangelical theological college at Cambridge, for the love of its saintly but very conservative principal, Handley Moule (C. F. D. Moule's great-uncle), whose views on eternal life (and especially no doubt on eternal death) he approved, it is said, against 'the larger hope' of Dean Farrar, the author of *Eric, or Little by Little.* Yet here was the man who ended up the close friend of the Benedictine monks at Downside and a representative along with Halifax and Frere at the Malines Conversations between the Church of England and the Church of Rome. Indeed he was appealed to by the Anglo-Catholics as their ally on apostolic succession and the Western rite. Yet he was never their man or indeed any party's man. In a letter to a friend in Convocation at the time of the 1928 Prayer Book controversy he wrote,

> I am appalled at the formulated concessions to what calls itself

> Anglo-Catholicism. The Bishops have despaired of ruling their flocks on the inherited principles of a sober Anglicanism. . . . It is doctrine that has got wrong. . . . It will make some immense difference to them whether they do or do not receive Holy Communion before they die. Such a teaching would have been quite unintelligible in the religious circle in which I was brought up. And I can hardly conceive anything more remote from the intention of the Last Supper and the early eucharist of the Church.

It was his absorption in New Testament study that had led him (as later it led me through my work on *The Body*) to his high doctrine of the church as 'the divinely appointed instrument for the unity of the human race in Christ', which was the leading doctrine also of Westcott. This conservative evangelical had also contributed the article on 'the Church', among many others, to the radical *Encyclopaedia Biblica*; and when he was appointed to Westminster the church paper *The Guardian* did not know whether to call him a high churchman with broad sympathies or a broad churchman with high sympathies!

But I must pass from Armitage, the most complex and cantankerous of the brothers, much more rapidly to the others. Another, John, who confusingly went up to Christ's with the same initials the same year and got a first in theology and a blue for cross-country running, offered himself, after teaching for a time at a school in Heidelberg, to the Church Missionary Society, in whose service he was to die on the Niger after beginning the first translation of the New Testament into Hausa. He seems to have caught the worst of the conservative evangelical's intolerance and was what today we should recognize as a hard-liner, not least towards the great but easy-going black Bishop Crowther. He was to be followed there at the call of sacrifice by his brother Charles, who survived the most arduous journeys with incredible physical stamina and lived to complete, and see through many revisions, the first dictionary of the Hausa language and numerous other books. His later years were spent as editorial secretary of the other, high-church, Anglican missionary society, the Society for the Propagation of the Gospel, where he pioneered a considerably more daring approach to missionary literature and other faiths than contemporary churchmanship allowed, and which was to lead in the next generation to the *International Review of Missions*.

Forbes through his *Letters to his Friends*, published posthumously by Charles and one of the spiritual classics of the twentieth century, could be said perhaps to have influenced more people more deeply than any of the others. Indeed by the sheer power of friendship and prayer he was the inspiration, Charles Raven once insisted to me, that led to the Cambridge College chaplaincy system, on which even now Oxford is only just catching up! Yet it is often forgotten that he was very much an academic in his own right, succeeding Armitage as Dean of Christ's, a scholar among other fields in Coptic and the philosophy of religion, in Christian doctrine and church history, and winning more University prizes than them all – and no less than four of the brothers won the Carus Greek Testament prize, Armitage interestingly *not* included, since he read classics and not theology. I have Hort's mark-sheet of a year my father entered when there were no less than seventeen candidates from Trinity alone, though Hort's comments on some are pretty caustic. When I was an examiner exactly a hundred years later there was one from the whole university!

But I must not forget the sisters. Two, as I said, were deaconesses. One, Cecilia, who had never had any formal schooling and also died tragically early of tuberculosis, nevertheless wrote a pioneering study on *The Ministry of Deaconesses* (with an introduction by Randall Davidson and an erudite appendix by Armitage), which reveals a width and depth of learning in church history and liturgy which I doubt has since been matched by the advocates in our generation of women's priesthood. The other, Bessie, wrote the life of Head Deaconess Gilmour, the founder of their work in South London. Florence, whose student copy of Lightfoot's *Apostolic Fathers* I still use, was never ordained, but was heavily engaged in pastoral and literary work and wrote the life of her brother Charles – also with a foreword by Randall Davidson. (Davidson seems to have been a great writer of forewords – he also contributed one to T. R. Glover's *Jesus of History* – as was William Temple after him. A publisher once told Alec Vidler he had six manuscripts in his office with forewords by Temple – five of them unpublishable!) But Davidson was a close friend of both sides of my family and indeed conducted my parents' wedding. He used to stay with Armitage at Wells before Easter – the only time, it was said, that the Dean, who ruined his health by working into the small hours on cups of tea and cigarettes, was ever seen at the weekday early service!

In all this I have not yet spoken of Arthur, my father, whom prejudice perhaps leads me to regard as the most complete Church of England man of all. He had been brought up to value as deeply as any of them the piety of his evangelical heritage, whose 'reality and attractiveness', he said in an address to an Irish audience shortly before his death, 'were above and beyond all doubt and suspicion'. But as a student he came to see, under the influence of the great Cambridge triumvirate, that it was combined with 'a great deal of rather timid intellectual anxiety and misgiving'. Nevertheless at the age of 37 he was still writing to his sister Florence, of 'the family tradition which Mother so calmly embodies', that 'I can never get into close contact with any persons to whom it is entirely unknown'. Yet that was in the course of a letter helping her to come to terms with what she was evidently beginning to sense in the very different tradition of a religious order.

> I am grieved that you should feel that others of the family are not likely to understand and sympathise with you. For myself I can truly say that no presentation of the religious life has ever moved me more profoundly than that which you have lately been seeing and many and many a time I have felt that I must abandon myself wholly to accept and follow it.

If he had I should presumably never have been born!

But it was not only within the spectrum of Anglican churchmanship that he yearned to embrace and hold together what was best in every tradition. In an earlier letter he had written to the same sister:

> In regard to religious differences, we [Anglicans] want to have all that is true to both the Unitarian and the Roman Catholic and it is the glory of our middle position that we may: only we lose the definiteness, perhaps, that comes of exclusiveness and this sometimes seems a strength.

But only 'seems'. For he was essentially a man of inclusiveness rather than of exclusiveness or party faction. After his death it was said of him by a fellow proctor in the Convocation of Canterbury, where his words were few but weighty: 'Any speech which seemed to narrow the comprehensiveness of the Church of England, or to hinder the work of reunion, was fairly certain to bring him to his feet.'

My father was the eldest but one of the family, and after the death in the same year of his father and of his elder brother George (but lately ordained to a Lancashire curacy and yet more recently married) he had the onerous task of bringing up the large family. Refused ordination by Frederick Temple on account of his eyesight (he got his first in theology at Cambridge by dictating to his brother

John in the Senate House!), he had started as his father's curate in Liverpool. So with his death his job ceased too. Yet somehow they all managed to survive. Though he too was a scholar (he was a candidate for the Lady Margaret Chair when Inge got it) and was widely read in science and philosophy, as well as editing Tennyson's *In Memoriam* for the University Press, he gave his life primarily to mission-work and pastoral theology. He headed the College of Mission Clergy in London and the war-time National Mission for Archbishop Davidson, before being appointed by him Canon of Canterbury – which is where I began. But what interests me here is that long before the latter's revival as a cult-figure in Anglican theology he was a disciple of F. D. Maurice, whose signed portrait now hangs in my study and whose influence shines through letters he wrote while still in his twenties. And Maurice of all the nineteenth-century figures in the Church of England was *the* non-party man who epitomized that passion both for theological freedom and for social responsibility which I shall be going on to characterize as the twin pillars of the Anglican ethos in which I most deeply believe. And in the title of his last published book my father described the distinctive role of the Anglican Communion to be the church of *The New Learning and the Old Faith* – which is a combination to which I warm.

'Thou has set my feet in a large room', or in the striking if less euphonious version of the Jerusalem Bible, 'You have given my feet space and to spare.' It is this space in which to spread and to serve on which I want to focus in the second and third lectures. But let me devote what remains of this one to exploring further both constructively and critically the room in which I have been born and nurtured. Its large and free spirit was I think well described by Charles Davis in the course of an address explaining why he did *not* join the Anglican church on leaving the priesthood of the Roman Catholic. 'Both my wife and myself', he said, 'have learnt to recognize the distinctive flavour of that discreet, unoppressive friendship common among Anglicans, with their exceptional tolerance and sensitivity for divergent personal convictions.' There are many ways in which one could seek to designate this pervasive but elusive quality. Like most important things it is a good deal easier to say what it denotes than what it connotes, to point to it rather than define it. There is the familiar opening to the Preface to the Prayer Book: 'It hath been the wisdom of the Church of England to keep the mean between the two extremes, of too much stiffness in refusing, and of too much easiness in admitting any variation from it', with its echo in the charge to a bishop on his consecration: 'Be so merciful, that you be not too remiss; so minister discipline, that you forget not mercy.' Or there is the typically Anglican prayer, which in giving thanks for 'the Holy Catholic Church, the mother of us all who bear the name of Christ' speaks of 'the mercies by which it hath *enlarged* and comforted the souls of men'. And to that I would dare to add some words from one of my father's books: 'Large souls do not try to impose themselves upon us. . . . In their presence we spread, and feel strangely at home.'

It is no accident that the sources of these quotations, except the last, have been prayers or the Prayer Book, rather than, say, the Thirty-Nine Articles of Religion, however much they reflect the same *via media* between Romanism and Calvinism, delineating freedom rather than defining dogma. For in our communion above all it has been the *lex orandi*, the rule of prayer, that has shaped the *lex credendi*, the rule of faith. It has been a praying, pastoral, though *also* a learned, ministry which has been our chief glory. Yet it is the proportion of faith and order, rather than anything distinctive of our own, that has been most characteristic. As Geoffrey Fisher once said, 'We have no doctrine of our own.' It has been *how* we have believed which has marked us out, though not marked us off. In the manuscript of an as yet unpublished life of Armitage my eye was caught by the marks of the Anglican way which (said its author, the Revd T. F. Taylor) his 'cautious reverence', inherited from Westcott and Hort, so largely exhibited. He characterized them, well I think, as 'reserve, a constant recurrence to first principles, fidelity to the evidence, and breadth of view'. Our concept of authority (and we find ourselves reaching for the *word* less than many) has not been single or rigid but of a threefold cord, strong in its supple combination, of scripture, tradition and reason. We have declined to isolate the infallible man or the infallible book or the epynomous founder. The 'complete Church of England man' has always been a composite and a rounded character (which doesn't necessarily mean complex and rotund!), a both-and man rather than an either-or, Catholic *and* Reformed, priestly *and* prophetic, profound *and* simple, inclusive by temperament rather than exclusive. One thinks of a Hooker or a Herbert, of a Maurice or a Westcott, or in our day of William Temple, who accepted me (far too lightly, as his custom was) for ordination (he himself ironically had at first been refused, and his father had refused my father!) or of George Bell, whose episcopal robes I am humbled to wear.

So one could go on extolling the many-faceted splendours of the

Church of England – till in complacency one had lost all touch with reality. 'When I speak of religion', said Fielding's Pastor Thwackum with the sublime confidence of the eighteenth century, 'I mean the Christian religion. And when I speak of the Christian religion, I mean the Protestant religion. And when I speak of the Protestant religion, I mean the Church of England'! I cannot believe that such triumphalism is a serious temptation today. What is easier is to preen ourselves on our 'comprehensiveness' without realizing that it is in every sense a *stupor mundi*, an object of incredulous disbelief to the world and even our fellow-Christians, or on our position as a 'bridge church' without sensing the barriers that go up when anyone, like the Methodists for instance, might actually try to walk across it. It is possible for an Anglican to sit back and watch the ecumenical tide and persuade himself that it's all coming our way – the Catholics are becoming more reformed and the Reformed are becoming more Catholic, which (of course) is what *we've* always been. Indeed one of the charges in a symposium called *American Catholic Exodus*, which was a full-blooded riposte from the right, was that 'they', the reformers of Vatican II, have 'reproduced Anglicanism within the Body of the Church' – which sounds splendid till you realize that what is meant is that 'they have broken us into a high Church and low Church whose respective members scarcely speak to one another any more'! As a matter of fact I don't think this *is* the greatest danger these days. It is when high and low get together solely on what they are against, whether it is Methodist unity or divorce discipline or women priests. When Herod and Pilate agree on *anything* I *know* the truth must lie elsewhere – and the middle ground of a reasonable religion gets squeezed out.

I cannot resist throwing in at this point the reply of one of my pupils years ago at Wells Theological College (who has since died in tragic circumstances) when asked on a bishop's form 'What is your churchmanship?' – and if you ask a silly question you deserve a silly answer. 'Central-low-broad', he put down. Pressed to elucidate, he replied: 'Central is what I think I am, and what everybody in the Church of England thinks they are. Low is what other people think I am. Broad means that I don't know – and don't care a damn anyhow'!

But amusing as this may be (and I think *fundamentally* sound) it looks to those outside a symptom as much of our disease as of our health, of our weakness as of our strength. It is in every sense *The Integrity of Anglicanism*, to use Stephen Sykes's self-critical title, that they question. To see ourselves as others see us has not always been the greatest of Anglican gifts. And it comes as a shock to the pride of our comprehensiveness that *one* of the reasons Charles Davis gave for not joining the Anglican Church was that from his working-class, and in a previous generation Baptist, background no one would have felt at home in such a class-show.

What sort of a room is this large room in which our feet have been set? It has indeed served the saints for many functions – for dining and celebrating, for studying and talking, and taking their rest. But if there is one room in the house with which I suppose people would instinctively identify it, it is the drawing-room. The Anglican drawing-room, gracious, well-proportioned, urbane: it was this that it was John Wesley's crime to desecrate, by unseemly 'enthusiasm'. And for increasing numbers today it is reverting to its original meaning – the withdrawing room, the saloon bar of the religious club.

We cannot continue at ease in it without facing many questions. There are those who are requiring us to accept the challenge of open-plan living. Separate rooms, even with unlocked doors, seem a growing anachronism in the house of God. Shared churches, ecumenical team-ministries, must at any rate in newer areas be the order of the day. Of course the cost of adaptation, physically and mentally, is high. But the well-intentioned preservation societies (and the plaque of what was then 'The Leicester Permanent Building Society' opposite Great St Mary's at Cambridge, said a friend of mine, was the former Bishop of Leicester's image of the Church of England!) appear to forget that there may be fewer and fewer of the next generation wanting to live in such edifices, however redolent of antiquity. And the Methodist parlour is often now if anything more musty than the Anglican drawing-room.

But there are also those who question, more radically, whether we should be living in a permanent house at all. Indeed Charles Davis's fundamental reason for declining to become an Anglican was that he didn't want simply to exchange the burden of one piece of ecclesiastical masonry for another. Shelter there must be for the people of God, structures and organizations – and good ones – for its functioning in the world of principalities and powers. But let these never obscure the fact that it is a pilgrim people composed of those (as the Passover rubric required) who must be on their way in the morning. The Christian Church, we should not forget, was born in 'a large upper room' and its characteristic (and very Anglican) local expression 'the parish' comes from the word *paroikos*, the temporary resident without citizen's rights, who was seen by the author of I Peter (2.11) and by the writer of the Epistle to Diognetus (5 and 6) as the type of the Christian in the world.

We have a goodly heritage in a fair ground: never let us be guilty of decrying or despising it – nor of deriding it as a fair-ground. 'Honour your father and mother' is, as St Paul observed, 'the first commandment with a promise attached' (Eph. 6.2) – and there is much blessing in it. Yet the Anglican ethos has been shaped in a slower world than ours. It is like the Cambridge college lawn whose secret was being given to an overseas visitor: 'Oh, there's nothing to it. You roll and you mow, and you mow and you roll, and you just go on doing that for 400 years.' It happens however that the King's lawn of which I heard that told is a mid-Victorian creation – and that is only too true also of much in Anglicanism, including, as I said, that name.

Anglicans have deep roots. They think instinctively in organic terms. They have made much of the church as the body of Christ – Armitage's *Ephesians* is a quintessentially Anglican commentary. They are more at home with teleology than eschatology, with evolution than revolution. Yet it is precisely their depth of root that gives them in my experience the freedom to be radicals, which means as I understand it men and women who go to the roots. The greatest potential contribution of the Anglican today is, I believe, this freedom, this courage to be – and to become. It is a freedom grounded in much richness of soil, but flexible enough to adapt to rapid social change, glorying in the risk and the openness of the situation he faces. 'Thou hast set my feet in a large room.' But what is the purpose of feet? The American was gazing from his driving seat at Westminster Abbey. 'Why don't you get out?', said his wife; 'What do you think the Lord has given you two feet for?' 'Oh, one for the brake, the other for the gas pedal.' Yet the purpose of feet is to walk – if necessary out of the room. For within our Father's house are many resting places. And finally in the city and kingdom of God there will be no temple at all.

After this first lecture at St John's Auckland I was asked what were the implications of what I was saying for those who could claim no 'roots'. The question came from one who was heard to say, 'It's all very well for him. But I am an orphan, and all I know about my parents is that they were descended from convicts in Australia.' It seemed a question which demanded a careful reply.

It is certainly no part of the gospel to say that unless you have roots you cannot be a starter. That was the answer of those who took their stand on the fact that they were the children of Abraham – and the rest nowhere. This received equally short shrift from John the Baptist, from Jesus and from Paul (and there are not too many things on which we have evidence that their teaching was completely at one!). 'God can make children for Abraham out of these stones' (Matt. 3.9; Luke 3.8) – and stones have no roots at all!

Yet having said that as strongly as one can, it is also worth remembering all of us have roots. None of us was born yesterday. Indeed Haley's *Roots* is precisely about the seemingly most rootless flotsam and jetsam on earth – slaves whose roots had been deliberately and cruelly severed and their very names changed so as to cut their links with the past. Ironically too in New Zealand the most rootless persons are among the white, *pakeha* majority. The Maoris, though borne across the seas from scattered islands over many generations, retain the strongest possible awareness of their genealogy, which tells them who they are and is literally built into the decoration of their meeting-places.

In Romans 9–11 St Paul is speaking, as Hebrew son of Hebrew parents, about his own roots, which significantly he refuses to disown or disparage. Yet he is addressing Gentiles who had no part in the root and sap of the olive. They had been 'strangers to the community of Israel, outside God's covenants and the promise that goes with them' (Eph. 2.12). His gospel is *not* that they have to become Jews in order to be Christians (or *mutatis mutandis* Englishmen in order to become Anglicans!). That was the answer of the Judaizers by whom he was opposed even more bitterly than by the Jews. Nevertheless in Christ the blessing, the inheritance of Abraham, *is* theirs. In him who is the 'issue' of Abraham's seed (Gal. 3.16), the scion of David's stock (Rom. 1.3), they have been engrafted, and that by sheer grace – not to become Jews but to become one in the Christ in whom there is neither Jew nor Greek. The Jews have no advantage – only the deeper responsibility. The gospel is that nothing turns on natural heritage. There is no standing here, no ground of pride – it is all 'so much garbage' (Phil. 3.8). And yet the gospel is that we Gentiles are *given* roots: all the fullness of Israel is ours – and let no man dare to treat it lightly.

But the final answer to those who feel rootless and therefore worthless is that this is true not only of the Christian but of Christ. However one takes the stories of his birth, Jesus was apparently (and no Christian would have invented this) without a father to give him his name. In a patriarchal culture he was known, according to Mark (6.3), as 'the son of Mary', and that was a most shaming appellation. And Matthew in his genealogy (and genealogy was as fundamental to the Jew as to the Maori) is evidently acutely conscious of the fact that according to the Law of Moses no child of an irregular union could be a member of God's people, let alone its Messiah. Yet he does not attempt to deny the irregularity, as later he denies Jewish slanders about his resurrection. He boldly accepts it as being 'of God' and goes out of his way to drag in (for they are in no way essential to the line traced through the male) four other women whose dubious liaisons God has overruled (Matt. 1.1–16). The gospel for him, as for Paul, is that nothing depends on the righteousness of the law, but everything on the 'putting right' of grace. So at the express initiative of God Joseph, as a 'son of David', is directed to give the child his name, and thus engraft him into the people of God and the richness of the messianic line (1.18–25). Even for Christ this is of grace, not right. It is, as St Paul put it, 'against all nature' (Rom. 11.24). Even Jesus, one may say, is 'justified by faith', the faithfulness of Joseph, who was prepared to believe God against all that 'principle' would suggest.

Roots are neither for boasting nor for despising. And they are necessary for fruit. 'Make the tree good' insists Jesus (Matt. 12.33) – 'for you do not pick grapes from briars nor figs from thistles' (Matt. 7.16). There is nothing against nature there! Yet this making good is not of human effort or pedigree. All is of God. Yet it includes rather than negates the blessing of Abraham – and the obedience of Mary and the trustfulness of Joseph, against everything that his eyes saw and his culture told him.

2. THEOLOGICAL FREEDOM

The church's experience of heresy trials in recent times has not exactly been a happy one. In fact like imprisonment for African politicians it has almost become a *sine qua non* for advancement! Thus, and here I quote John Macquarrie (from a report I shall be mentioning shortly):

> In 1856 John McLeod Campbell published *The Nature of the Atonement*, now universally recognized as one of the classics of Scottish theology. Twenty-five years earlier this great but unfortunate man had been deposed from the ministry of the Church of Scotland. His 'error' was that, in his preaching, he taught that God's forgiveness and reconciling grace are offered to all men, not just to a predestined few.

This was deemed by an overwhelming majority of the General Assembly to be 'at variance with the Word of God and the standards of the Church of Scotland'. Similarly F. D. Maurice, now recognized as perhaps the most representative Anglican theologian of the nineteenth century, was dismissed from his chair at the Anglican foundation of King's College, London, for being 'unsound' on eternal punishment – though his dangerous contacts with the Christian Socialists did not exactly help. My own university of Cambridge, I am glad to say, subsequently offered him the chair of Moral Philosophy, and he ministered with distinction as Chaplain of St Edward's Church. The only bishop of the Church of England to have been put on trial before the Archbishop of Canterbury since the Reformation was Edward King, Bishop of Lincoln, in 1889. Forty-six years later he was accorded the nearest thing to canonization in the Anglican church when at a commemoration service he was described by a subsequent archbishop, Cosmo Gordon Lang, as 'Edward King: Bishop and Saint'. A few years back I was guest-lecturer for Albert Geyser in Johannesburg, who had been offered the chair of New Testament studies at Witwatersrand University immediately after being convicted of heresy by the Dutch Reformed Church. He was accused of having an 'Arian' Christology, but his real 'error' again was that he confuted the theology of *apartheid*. And so one could go on – though New Zealand has its own example to hand, even though the heresy charge did not stick, in Dr Lloyd Geering, who is now the only University Professor of Religious Studies in the country and has just produced an important new book, *Faith's New Age*.

But saner counsels look as if they have begun to prevail (at least in the Anglican Communion) and when an attempt was made in 1966 to start proceedings against Bishop James Pike, the Protestant Episcopal Church of the United States was fortunate in having in John Hines a wise presiding bishop. He appointed to advise him a theological committee chaired by Bishop Stephen Bayne, the first Executive Officer of the Anglican Communion, of whom Sydney Evans, the Dean of Salisbury and himself an archetypal Anglican, has recently spoken in *Theology* (March 1979) as inviting comparison with the seventeenth-century divines for his understanding of the Anglican vision and vocation. Within a year this committee produced a report which should be required reading for anyone trying to understand the Anglican ethos today. It is from its title, *Theological Freedom and Social Responsibility*, that I have taken the headings for these last two lectures. I became involved in it because I was asked to submit evidence, which struck me at the time as rather like the poacher turned game-keeper. For only a few years earlier there were plenty who would have been happy to see me arraigned! In fact there was never any question of this, and the most I got was what I suppose you would call an official archiepiscopal 'rebuke', which Michael Ramsey has been generous enough to say personally and publicly a number of times since showed a certain over-reaction. Indeed I have often testified to the fact that in no other organization, religious or secular, would I have been so free. And because it is so difficult to be thrown out of the Church of England I have over the years felt a special responsibility to those I have known who have suffered such a fate in other communions.

I remember defending James Pike himself in his own diocese of California before I had ever met him, or I myself was suspect, when he ran into some flak over the doctrine of the Trinity. Subsequently we became good friends – and who couldn't have loved this lovable but exasperating man? – despite the fact that he dedicated perhaps his worst book to me and Paul Tillich! I repaid the compliment by dedicating my own *Christian Freedom in a Permissive Society* to this 'seeker and contender for freedom and truth' who died tragically the week before the book was finished. We were often twinned by the media, yet I think our concerns were subtly different. This comes out in the difference between his title *A Time for Christian Candor* and my *Honest to God*. Candour is about saying what you mean, honesty about meaning what you say. But with neither of us was there any intention not to say what the church says – which I take to be the real criterion of heresy. It was simply, to use a phrase I remember from a German student at the time, that there are moments when in order to be for the church you have to be against it.

The Committee's report was the best thing to come out of a sorry affair. On the one hand, it fully agreed with John Knox, another of its witnesses, that the church must reject certain kinds of teaching, not because they are 'wrong' in verbal comparison with some written formula, but because they strike at 'the life of the community itself', emptying its distinctive categories of 'their rich and perennial existential meaning' and leaving them not 'inexhaustible symbols of a transcendent and very present reality, but mere shells reminding men of an earlier faith'. But it also represented a vigorous defence of theological freedom, and made its own some words from my evidence:

> All exploration, whether in the theological or the social field, involves the risk, indeed the certainty, of mistakes. But it is at least arguable, from the study of church history, that more damage has almost always been done in the long run by the suppression of opinion than by any error given rein by freedom. At any rate the church must act on the assumption, till proved otherwise, that freedom will in any instance be less harmful than the attempt to curb it.

To that I would add some words of M. M. Thomas from India:

> One-sidedness and error are characteristic of all living theology. Indeed in the past the 'heretic' (defined as one-sided) has often been a better Christian and invariably a better evangelist than others who held to orthodox definitions of the faith. This was and is so still, because he is on a particular frontier in dialogue with the world of men there. There is something wrong in such a definition of orthodoxy and heresy.

This is indeed a point that I made in my evidence to the Committee and perhaps I may be allowed to repeat its closing paragraph:

> There is implicit in the category of heresy, at any rate as popularly understood, the assumption that the final bar of Christian truth is the church and its juridical authority. But if theological inquiry and social criticism are properly part of the church's prophetic ministry, this can never be the complete truth. The prophet is answerable not simply to the church but to the kingdom. Congruence with the church's formulations is only one aspect by which prophetic activity must be judged. Indeed, there are many instances, especially in the area of social criticism, where witness to the kingdom has meant witness *against* the church in the name of the world. The prophet has historically often been most free when he has been protected against the church and has enjoyed relative independence of ecclesiastical authority. And this is being felt by many to be more rather than less true today, as the church wrestles with a genuinely engaged theology of the secular. Both social critics and theological inquirers are sensing that they can speak with an authentic voice only if they have at least one foot, economically and academically, within the structures of the world. To be completely answerable to the religious institution is to be living, so it seems to many today, in something less than genuine solidarity with men

out of which alone the prophet can be heard. 'Heresy', therefore, comes to appear of increasingly limited relevance as an adequate or final criterion of Christian truth. For where, within the secular order, is the bar to be found at which thought or action may be judged heretical? To invoke the category is to appeal to a standard which must itself be questioned.

This brings me to the heart of what I want to say in relation to the specifically Anglican concern for truth and freedom. There are those who are questioning – and questioning very healthily – 'the integrity of Anglicanism'. What *does* Anglican comprehensiveness stand for? Are there any limits to its freedom, or is this running out into undifferentiated and indisciplined licence? These are serious questions, and they raise the issue, to use another title, this time of John Knox's, of the *Limits of Unbelief*. But this very phrase makes me want to stop and ask, Are we being betrayed into defining freedom by its limits, by its edges rather than its centre? This question is raised, for instance, by the relation between freedom and authority. These are popularly conceived as opposites. Authority 'comes down' on freedom, say, to publish, as it did so notoriously and so disgracefully in the case of Teilhard de Chardin. Yet this very polarization betrays a distortion. For authority and freedom are but two sides of the same coin.

Jesus we are told spoke 'with authority'. And this is the gospels' way of saying with Barth and Van Buren that he was the truly free man. He spoke not, like the scribes, from authorities but from source, from the centre rather than from the edges by which lesser men buttress their opinions. It is to be observed how the various words in this field cluster around the idea of origin. The Greek for 'authority', *exousia*, literally means 'from being', while the Latin *auctoritas* comes from *auctor*, author, and behind that from *augere*, to grow, as in inaugurate. 'Authenticity' interestingly has a different root, but again from the centre, this time from the Greek *autos*, the self. 'Origin', like 'orient', comes from *oriri*, to arise; and 'order', closely twinned with authority in 'law and order', from a word of the same root, *ordire*, to begin (as in exordium). So one could go on. These are 'centre' words, and one of the characteristic features of Jesus's teaching was to push men back to source. 'At the beginning', *en archē*, in principle, 'it was not so' (Mark 10.6); at heart, in its inwardness, divorce is adultery, covetousness idolatry, and so on. Typical is his truly 'radical' saying, going to the roots as the rabbis would not have dared: 'The sabbath was made for man, not man for the sabbath' (Mark 2.27). Or take his reply to the question put by the lawyer: 'And who is my neighbour?' This is a question of definition, of edges, of setting limits (from the Latin *fines*). It is really saying, 'Who is *not* my neighbour?', as in the Israeli religious education slogan I saw by the Wailing Wall in Jerusalem: 'Love thy fellow-Jew as thyself' – though apparently not thy fellow-Arab. But Jesus's answer is to force the matter back to the centre, with another question: 'Who *was* neighbour, who *proved* neighbour?' (Luke 10.29–37). The neighbour is thus defined not in terms of the other but of the self, not of the edges but of the centre. If the heart is right, the boundaries will look after themselves: in fact they will fall away, as they did on the Jericho road.

Freedom and order, freedom and authority, are correlates, not opposites. Each is part of the definition of the other. One is not true at the expense of the other, so that the more freedom the less order, and *vice versa*. That is what happens when the polarity becomes a polarization, and order is defined in terms of the limits of freedom. But both belong properly to the centre, to the *auctor* or *ordo*. Writing of the *fons et origo* of church order, H. E. W. Turner once described the twelve as the 'right markers' of the New Israel, those round whom it forms and on whom it turns, the *cardo* or hinge of the church militant (hence, later, 'cardinals'). Equally 'heresy' properly defined, at the centre not the edges, means in origin 'choice' or chosen path. So St Paul said to Felix: 'I am a follower of the way, which they call a *hairesis*' (Acts 24.14). In its inwardness there is 'heresy' only when the choice is genuinely different – not when certain lines are transgressed.

Yet it is this latter picture which is prominent in another cluster of words now more usually associated with authority. Keeping order is conceived in terms of policing boundaries, patrolling, or going the rounds. ('Patrol' comes from the French for 'paddling about in the mud'! Etymological dictionaries are for me a source of endless fascination.) Freedom is thereby defined, marked off, in terms of 'limits' (from *limes*, a threshold) to 'licence' (what is 'licit' or allowed). There is a 'line' (literally, a thread, as in 'linen') which says, 'Thus far and no further.' Consider the associations of such phrases as 'drawing the line', 'holding the line', 'toeing the line', 'coming into line', 'signing on the line'. The line determines what's in and what's out, and who's in and who's out. The extreme example of this hardening of the edges is the mentality of the *laager*, formed by the ring of ox-wagons, in which in my experience fundamentalists are never happier (that's why I always refuse to put them on the defensive). Their fundamentals lie in theory at the centre; but they defend them by strengthening the edges, which is a sign of insecurity rather than of security. Yet right through church history the preoccupation with edges has left its mark. Consider, for instance, the importance attached to the notion of 'canon', which simply means a ruled line.

It was used first of scripture. The original idea was to affirm what was closest to source, truly apostolic, in direct touch with the living voice. Yet quickly the story of the canon became a concern for edges, revolving around what was to be included and what excluded. And the notion of a fixed canon was invoked to safeguard 'the deposit once and for all delivered to the saints'. Hence the concept of 'holy scripture', of the Bible with a belt.

Then the word became attached to the ministry. It even designates an office in the church – 'the reverend Mr Ruled Line'. And the limits of 'holy orders' became vital with the establishment of the church under Constantine. When the Christian priesthood took over the role and perquisites of the pagan priesthood it became necessary to decide who was eligible to enjoy 'benefit of clergy' and who not. Hence the entrenching of a 'clergy line' down the middle of the diverse ministries of the Spirit. In the New Testament *clēros* and *laos* are names for the same thing – the whole priestly people of God.

All this threw into relief the use of the term in law. For the canons of the church are not only people but rules and regulations. The first canon law, like the first use of the term from which 'dogma' derives ('it seemed good (*edoxen*) to the Holy Spirit and to us'), is to be found in Acts 15, where the Council of Jerusalem, while allowing freedom from circumcision at the centre, 'drew the line' at things which would needlessly offend Jewish susceptibilities (15.28f). And that is where rules and regulations properly have their place – on the growing but constantly shifting edges. As I sat through the interminable debates of Convocation revising the canons of the Church of England, (*a*) I raised my hand instantly whenever there was a motion that 'this canon be deleted' (without asking which), and (*b*) I comforted myself by reflecting that within ten years of the Council of Jerusalem Paul was drawing quite a different line about the eating of meats sacrificed to idols in the dominantly Gentile culture of Corinth. I expect the new canons of the Church of England have worn just about as well – all I know is that as a bishop I never looked at them again.

But, finally, there was the canon of the mass, which from being the central and indeed the only prayer of the president of the eucharist, of which the Didache (10.7) said that the prophets were to 'give thanks as much as they desire', became the symbol of fixity and uniformity. Liturgical variations might be tolerated elsewhere, but of the canon it was pre-eminently (and still is even in the most flexible of rites) the authorized form, or forms, 'and no other'.

It is not surprising therefore that when it came to defining Anglicanism, as an 'ism' rather than an ethos, it should have been by the edges rather than the centre, by the lines that mark it off. Indeed since 1888 there have been four recognized lines – the sides of the famous Lambeth Quadrilateral. (This gives Anglicans an agreeable sense of being secure in Zion, four-square as the city of God itself!) These are the Scriptures, the Creeds, the Sacraments and the Historic Ministry. But patrolling them has become ever more of a messy business, and on all sides it seems increasingly difficult to draw the line (except an excessively dotted one) or to give a clear definition in terms of edges of 'what we stand for' (or should it be 'on'?). Hence the 'crisis in Anglicanism' so defined. If I had time I could go round the four and beat the bounds, a traditional Anglican parochial exercise until quite recently. But let me indicate very sketchily what I mean. For on all four sides what were once clear edges have become eroded or fuzzy.

i. Scripture

This was the Reformers' base-line. Nothing was to be required as necessary to salvation but what might be read therein or proved thereby. And for several centuries the infallibility of the Book could be assumed as confidently as the infallibility of the Pope (though the definition of each was a modern exercise). Listen to that staunch conservative Bishop Burgon giving the Bampton Lectures of 1861:

> The Bible is none other than the voice of Him that sitteth upon the throne. Every book of it, every chapter of it, every word of it, every syllable of it (where are we to stop?), every letter of it, is the direct utterance of the Most High. The Bible is none other than the Word of God, not some part of it more, some part of it less, but all alike the utterance of Him who sitteth upon the throne, faultless, unerring, supreme.

Who (even in the Diocese of Sydney!) could make those words his own today? From Liddon to Gore to Nineham, the various lines upon which it was thought possible to stand and fight have been out-flanked or abandoned. This does not mean that the centre will not hold. In fact I myself have returned a very positive answer to the question of my title, *Can We Trust the New Testament?*. But it is clear that the defences are not to be found on the perimeter. No one can set limits, Canute-like, to biblical criticism or to freedom of enquiry – as the greats of the Anglican tradition, like Lightfoot, Westcott and Hort, knew very well. Truth has to be trusted – in complete open-endedness.

ii. The Creeds

This again has been a traditional frontier on which Anglicans have stood. In fact uniquely in their worship they have sought to impose not two creeds but three (I have always thought the Athanasian Creed on St John the Baptist's day the ultimate in rubrical requirement!). *Pearson on the Creeds*, one of the Anglican classics, sits superbly bound, but I confess unread, on my shelves. 'Rehearse the articles of thy belief' was one of the requests of the Catechism to which unthinkingly I responded as a child. But today the relation between 'faith' and 'the Faith' is properly recognized to be less simple. And what of the limits of interpretation? Gore, with all his liberal catholicism, drew the line by insisting on literal acceptance of what he called the 'credal miracles' of the virgin birth and the resurrection. The Report of the Church of England Doctrine Commission under William Temple, a notable Anglican landmark for which Geoffrey Lampe has recently written a new and commendatory preface, allowed more latitude, and today what truth is to be understood as myth and what as fact is wide open. The subsequent report of the Doctrine Commission, *Christian Believing* (and the title, rather than *Christian Beliefs*, is itself significant), shows how much water has flowed under the bridges. And the terms of subscription to the subordinate Anglican standard, the Thirty-nine Articles, give a fair indication of the gradual loosening of assent. A new form of subscription was drawn up in 1865 and another in 1975, and few I am sure would want to go back on either. The centre is still affirmed as 'witnessed' to in 'the historic formularies of the Church of England', but no signature is required to the edges. In the process conscience is strengthened rather than weakened, and truth advanced. For, as St Paul said, 'anything which does not arise from conviction is sin' (Rom. 14.23).

iii. The Sacraments

Here again there is no doubt about the centre – baptism and the eucharist have never been more central to the Anglican worshipping community than they are today. Yet the lines are even more blurred – for instance between baptism and confirmation. As I grew up, one of the few universally understood lines of pastoral discipline (actually drawn more rigidly than by the Prayer Book itself with its 'ready and desirous to be confirmed') was that you could not receive communion until you had been confirmed (it was rather like premarital sex – though it is interesting to find my Victorian father urging his young sister to take communion if she was ready for it). Yet baptism rather than confirmation is increasingly coming to be seen, formally in the Episcopal Church of America and experimentally elsewhere, as the sensible basis for children to receive communion with the family. (I saw a mother the other day breaking off a bit of her wafer for her baby at the rail – and how natural and Christlike it seemed.) Moreover the traditional 'fencing' of Anglican altars (literally by Laud and mentally since) against those of other communions, on which we were still brought up till the sixties, has dramatically been abandoned, with no apparent catastrophic effects. In fact I remember sitting for three painful years on the Archbishops' Intercommunion Commission manoeuvring the barriers here a little, there a little, only to wake up one morning to discover that most of our Report was obsolescent when its ink had scarcely dried. While Geoffrey Fisher was urging the Methodists to take bishops into their system, unbelievably as it now seems in order to make intercommunion (not union) possible, Donald Coggan a generation later was, rightly, if unadvisedly, pressing the Pope for open communion, despite the fact that our orders are still officially 'null and void'! For it is only 'because of the one loaf' that most of these other issues of order and discipline will fall into place.

iv. The Ministry

Once again the Anglican Reformers thought they had here a clear and universally recognizable line. In the resonant words of the Preface to the Ordinal, 'It is evident unto all men diligently reading the Holy Scripture and ancient Authors, that from the Apostles' time there have been these Orders of Ministers in Christ's Church: Bishops, Priests, and Deacons'. Unhappily it is far from self-evident, and diligent attempts first to construct and then to maintain a pipeline of priestly succession over the head of the church have proved equally leaky and have largely been abandoned. And what is being affirmed in the sonorous phrase 'the historic episcopate'? Does it mean 'no bishop, no church', so that non-episcopal orders are as nugatory as Anglican ones are to papal? There is little support for that position, as Norman Sykes showed, in the classical Anglican divines of the seventeenth and eighteenth centuries. And in more recent times, from the Lambeth Conference appeal of 1920, through the traumas of the Church of South India debates of the fifties, the Anglican-Methodist discussions of the sixties, and the Covenanting for Unity and the Ten Propositions of the seventies, the situation has subtly but irrevocably changed. The centres have not been abandoned, yet the edges have been profoundly modified. And within the Anglican ministry itself the 'clergy line', not, that is, the functional one, organic to the New Testament, between the various offices and gifts of the Spirit but that between the clerisy and the rest, has been blurred by every new movement – by the declericalization of the liturgy, by the steadily growing numbers of priest-workers, earlier by the revival of deaconesses (the solemn fiction has been maintained that they are in 'orders' but not 'holy orders', 'ordained' yet sitting in the house of laity!) and more recently by the ordination of women-priests. Gad sir, where are we to draw the line? A voice was heard from one of the African bishops at the 1978 Lambeth Conference: 'We shall be discussing homosexuality next' – as if both were a sort of Western disease!

As one looks back on all these four lines, and others like them, the effect of what Stephen Sykes lumps together as 'liberalism' has been to erode, perforate and blur at every point. Defences have been breached, fences lowered, containers cracked. Are there no boundaries?, he asks, and, if not, is there any distinctiveness, and therefore integrity, left to Anglicanism? The sheep, it seems, are wandering on the mountains without a shepherd and without a fold. Or, in the lament of the Lord to Jeremiah, 'My tent is spoiled, and all my cords are broken: my children are gone forth of me, and they are not' (Jer. 10.20).

What is the answer? The instinctive response is in terms of Laud's characteristic prayer for the church: 'Where it is divided and rent asunder, make up the breaches of it, O thou Holy One of Israel.' Mend the fences, tighten the cords, define the doctrine, reinforce the discipline – and like Laud be thorough about it. This is the very understandable reaction of what one might call the 'law and order lobby'. And this is what we had in the Church of England under the post-war banner of 'putting our house in order' during the benign headmastership of Geoffrey Fisher – new canons, new catechisms, new psalters (though *not* creeds or articles), new translations of the Bible, new liturgies. And all this was entirely valid and desirable – not least the last two. There is a perfectly proper place for law – as long as it is at the edges and not at the centre. As Paul says in I Timothy (and here at least I believe the epistle is perfectly Pauline), 'We know that the law is an excellent thing, provided we treat it as law' (1.8), recognizing, that is, its role as a ring-fence against the lawless – but provided *per contra* that we do not set it at the centre and see it as the answer to putting man, or the church, right with God. The word of the gospel, as exemplified in the parable of the wicked husbandmen of Mark 12.1–12, is not to restore the hedge and rebuild the tower of the vineyard of the Lord of hosts ravaged in the parable of Isa. 5.1–7 on which it is grounded. It is that the owner sends his son, the son who sets us free. Or, in the words of the second Isaiah, the prophet of liberation, the message is not 'Tighten the cords and shorten the lines' but rather 'Enlarge the place of thy tent; . . . lengthen thy cords and strengthen thy stakes' (Isa. 54.2). And with this comes the call to return to the source of the water of life, to the freedom of the centre, to the strength and courage of inner integrity.

What the Bible is saying is 'Do not fear freedom' – in case the differentials are eroded, the lines obscured. A generation ago Roman Catholics were forbidden even to say the Lord's Prayer in public with other Christians for fear of what was called 'indifferentism' – that people might not know the difference or perhaps that their own flock might feel there was none. But that is the kind of fear that only love can cast out. As Shakespeare insisted,

> . . . to thine own self be true,
> And it must follow, as the night the day,
> Thou canst not then be false to any man.

'Love God', said St Augustine, 'and do what you like.' It sounds antinomian – against law – but it isn't. It is simply, with Jesus and Paul, reversing the order of code-morality, of cord-morality. I shall be returning to the field of ethics in the third lecture. But finally, some illustrations of how I believe this actually works out in the life and liberty of the church.

i. Liturgy

Twenty years ago we had in the diocese of Southwark, just before I joined it as Bishop of Woolwich, an ecclesiastical lock-out. Appalled by the indiscipline of the diocese, the new bishop, Mervyn Stockwood, issued not unreasonable regulations about the variations to be permitted from the service of 1662. Most parishes 'came into line', but one mission-church in particular refused to obey, and a padlock was literally placed on the door. That could not happen today, any more than we could settle our baptismal disputes like the Victorians by resort to the Privy Council. Why? Basically, because we have more freedom and correspondingly less licence. The situation has been transformed by enlarging our tents and by lengthening our cords rather than by shortening them. No one, I think, could have predicted the degree of consensus (and that doesn't mean unanimity) between all schools of churchmanship in the Church of England, and, as Lambeth 1978 revealed, in the Anglican Communion, which has formed round the new experimental services. (You can now hardly tell the Church of Ireland liturgy from the Roman Catholic!) There is much less uniformity, but much more unity. There is far greater variation of style and level – indeed *The Alternative Service Book 1980* of the Church of England contains five different eucharistic canons, whose criterion, I gather, was that all members of the Liturgical Commission could use them, whichever each or any might prefer on any one occasion. And the debate in General Synod was marked, from Anglo-Catholic and Evangelical alike, not only by charity but actually, I am told, by humour! And no one is saying, as the Romans have been betrayed into saying (in most un-Anglican fashion) over the Latin Mass, that whatever is not compulsory is forbidden. Those who prefer the liturgy of 1662 are entirely free to use it if they can find a consensus for it. The so-called Authorized Version of 1604 was never imposed – or even actually authorized. It found its level, and that after quite a time. 'Let both grow together till the harvest' (Matt. 13.30) and 'Let us wait and see if it be of God' (Acts 5.38f.) are good Anglican attitudes. And even the Reformers allowed Latin in college chapels – where they thought it would be understood!

ii. The Ordination of Women

This has been the most radical challenge to the integrity of the Anglican Communion since its re-formation. Traditionally we have enjoyed a large freedom of theology and wide variation of discipline within a common order. But now the order is apparently being breached. Is the past to be permitted not merely a vote but a veto? For it *is* a genuinely new thing. There is no real precedent for it, as opposed to ground for it, in scripture or tradition. Yet the question remains, Is God doing it? Or is it merely of men, inspired by the *Zeitgeist* rather than the gospel? The question is a litmus-test of Anglican attitudes. It is far from being the most important issue facing the church, but it may loom largest as the hump to be got over if we are to tackle, together, what really matters.

It was my privilege to be consultant to the group at the 1978 Lambeth Conference charged with this question, and it was a rare experience. The issue was not to debate the pros and cons of ordaining women: for by then the unthinkable had already happened – over considerable stretches of the Anglican Communion. The issue was, Could we live together with this challenge in integrity and truth? The group reflected a very fair cross-section of opinion and geographical distribution. I came to it with foreboding. But all I think would agree that we came out much more deeply united than we went in. This does not mean that we agreed, or even that we agreed to differ, but that there was a unity of the Spirit which not merely contained our differences but transformed them. And this was communicated not only to the larger section on Ministry but to the plenary session of the Conference, where resolutions were carried by an overwhelming majority, with not a single English bishop voting against (though three, I think, abstained), which were nevertheless sensed on both sides to be creative and founded on positive theological principle and not simply on compromise. I believe the Anglican Communion was stronger and richer as a result of that vote, in marked contrast with the spirit of fear and partisanship and untheological bumbledom that have prevailed in the subsequent debates in the General Synod of the Church of England, not least in the refusal of the House of Clergy even to receive validly ordained women from other provinces, which I believe is patently schismatic. Writing in advance of that decision the Editor of *Crockford's Clerical Directory* said in the Preface to the 1977–9 edition:

> Conceivably the Synod could refuse to allow Anglican women priests from overseas to celebrate the Holy Communion in England, and therefore imply a refusal to recognize non-Anglican women ministers; but at the moment we do not believe it possible that the Synod will be willing to inflict such damage on Anglican,

> as well as wider, unity in order to appease conservative groups in the Church of England which would in any case not be forced to invite women priests to minister in parishes under conservative control.

That the inconceivable happened within weeks of his writing this throws some doubt on his congratulations to the House of Clergy for their ecumenical maturity in voting against the Church of England itself ordaining women now!

Of course within the world-wide Anglican fellowship there are, and will continue to be for some time, at least two contradictory positions, but such a situation does not in my judgment add up, as it does for Stephen Sykes, to an exposure of the bankruptcy of Anglican comprehensiveness. It means that we have resolved to walk and grow, pray and work, together until we find some resolution and reconciliation – however painful and long that process may be. Does anyone *not* believe that under the Spirit we shall likewise, perhaps sooner than we thought, resolve the present sheer contradiction between our communions over Anglican and Roman Catholic orders? And does anyone doubt that this would come even more quickly if we were able to claim the forestalment of the Spirit by blessing and sharing the one bread, concelebrating if necessary through our divided ministries together? I firmly believe that in some such way, by giving and receiving, we *shall* integrate the ministries both of clergy and laity, male and female, between our separated churches and within them. And again in this as in other things I am inspired by hope (whose biblical correlate is endurance) rather than by optimism (whose secular basis is rosy prospects).

iii. Marriage discipline

I did not instance this under the sacramental lines that have become ragged and uncertain, but none is more so. *How*, under very varying and rapidly changing conditions, are we to maintain our witness to the Christian ideal – as *everyone* agrees we should? Is it by taking an absolutist stand, as still in theory in the Church of England, on whatever current line we deem tenable – no divorce (but perhaps extended annulment?); or no remarriage (especially for the clergy – or, if so, no benefice); or no remarriage in church (but blessing of secular weddings)? Or do we, like most other provinces now of the Anglican Communion, discriminate and discern between cases, recognizing that marriages are made for people, not people for marriages – and that marriages may die as well as people? Perhaps I may say what I did – ten to twenty years back when things were still more rigid – when consulted on this as a bishop (and my diocesan took just the same line). First, I was astonished who *did* consult me, conservative and high-church types for whom no one would have guessed that there would be any question of remarrying anyone in church. But, confronted by an actual pastoral situation, they were shaken: how could they show that persons were really more important than rules? So they rang me up for counsel and advice. I refused to direct them. I told them, This is what Convocation has said, this is what Parliament has said. You are free to marry them, or not to marry them. If you act responsibly, I will back what your conscience tells you you must do. If you want to use me to refuse, do so; if you run into trouble, either way, I will support you. But you, not I, know the unique pastoral situation and you must decide. And I can't remember having the slightest untoward come-back. I don't believe it led to indiscipline. I do believe it helped to create freedom. It was a second-best, because there ought to be an inbuilt but flexible structure of counselling and corporate discipline. But where the system refuses individuals must act – or persons are crushed.

iv. Doctrine

Again, I believe, as I said in a *Times* article on leaving Woolwich, the bishop's job, and authority's job in general, is primarily concerned with 'letting be'. And John Macquarrie has reminded us that we have a good precedent in the Author of all things, who is better described in terms not of pure being but of letting be. Authority is there to author freedom. I am not saying that at the edges there may not have to be sanctions. But I would still think that in the last resort these are better expressed wherever possible by letting go, with all pastoral concern and love. Jesus did not turn Judas out of the Last Supper, or even try to stop him leaving: 'he went out – and it was dark' (John 13.30). Similarly, says St John of the false teachers who were so divisive in his communities: 'they went out from among us' (I John 2.19). If so, so be it. If not so, then so be it also; and this may be harder to live with. This does not mean we do nothing: we may have to do a great deal, and few things are more expensive of pastoral care. But the appropriate response is one of affirming the positive, rather than motions of censure, which are usually counter-productive anyhow. One cannot say too strongly that the only answer ultimately to bad theology is better theology. Consider, for instance, one book published by a Bishop of the Church of England (and a former Fellow of Trinity to boot) which I think one must undoubtedly say was bad theology (or at any rate bad history) – and it wasn't *Honest to God* but E. W. Barnes's *Rise of Christianity*. If this rather sad book was a greater threat to the *ecclesia* than embarrassment to *academia*, which is doubtful, its errors were contained more effectively by its failure to win any serious body of scholarly support (and by such reasoned replies as that of C. H. Dodd) than by any archiepiscopal rebuke. This does not mean that church leaders should not seek to give responsible guidance, if only to make clear, alike in doctrine and in politics, the limits to which a man is committing the church as a whole – and if he is responsible he will make this clear himself, as I certainly tried to do in *Honest to God*.

Or take an example from an earlier generation. A slim volume was published in 1903 by my uncle Armitage called, modestly, *Some Thoughts on the Incarnation*. The substance of it reflects battle-lines – for instance, on the virgin birth – now largely left behind, but the prefatory letter to (not this time by) Archbishop Davidson contains, I think, some enduring wisdom. 'It is a fundamental principle', he wrote, 'that criticism must be met with criticism, not by counter-assertion.' 'Can anyone believe', he went on, 'that . . . the signature of the Bishop of Worcester to a joint episcopal declaration on this matter could effect anything at all for perplexed believers in comparison with the writings of Charles Gore?' (These were of course at that time the same person.) 'Interposing an utterance of authority' would, he urged, 'rouse intellectual resentment and will not allay disquiet.' Or, rather, one must say, it may indeed 'allay' it; for 'the faithful' (or should we say 'those of little faith'?) are always asking to be 'reassured'. But it will not resolve doubts if you do not listen to the questions – and that was the trouble with *The Truth of God Incarnate* as an 'answer' to *The Myth of God Incarnate*. If you want a model response to those who are 'disturbed' by a bishop's theology, read the passage from Augustine's *De Trinitate* (I. 2.4–5), quoted to great effect by Pike in his submission to the Committee – with its plea: 'Let us travel the road of love together.' And, if God is love, then as Temple insisted in the earlier Doctrine Report, 'To admit acrimony in theological discussion is itself more fundamentally heretical than any erroneous opinions upheld or condemned in the course of the discussion.'

But finally we should not forget three Pauline tests to be put to theological as to every other freedom: (a) Does my freedom cause my brother to stumble? (2) Does it build up or break down? (3) Can I say, in the words of the traditional lesson for the Epistle at the Consecration of Bishops: 'I have not shrunk from declaring to you the whole counsel of God' (Acts 20.27)?

'Fullness' and 'aliveness': these were two of the criteria advanced by the American report from which I started. And they grow at that quick centre which is Spirit. At the edges the law is there to protect (*not*, primarily, as I shall be saying later, to prevent). Yet you can so protect people that you cease to treat them as persons. So let me close with a last quotation from that report. After saying that freedom can, of course, be abused to cloak individualism, eccentricity and irresponsibility, it goes on:

> Nevertheless, to espouse freedom as a ruling principle entails a risk which the Church of all human associations must be the first to be willing to run. Why do we say this? Because the Church realizes that a faith which does not liberate cannot claim to be the authentic saving faith of Christ.

That is why theological freedom lies at the very heart of the gospel, and is such an unexpendable part of the birthright I cherish. As the signs gather of what Peter Hebblethwaite has called *The New Inquisition?*, I can only be thankful as an Anglican that I do not have anyone breathing down my neck like Küng nor any fear of being subjected to the sort of interrogation meted out to Schillebeeckx. It is a blessing for which I am prepared to pay a good deal in fuzzy edges!

3. SOCIAL RESPONSIBILITY

Now I want to turn from roots to fruits. Or rather I want to speak of the link between fruits and roots. For the fruits proclaim the roots. And the fruits of radical thinking and radical action are to be known by their roots. One of the groups condemned in the parable of the sower are those who 'have no root in themselves' (Mark 4.17). And there are those both in the church and in the world who make much show and noise of change but who have not the roots to feed or sustain it. The true radical cannot be *deraciné*.

So first I want to dig down a bit to the roots which have traditionally fed the characteristic Anglican commitment not only to theological freedom but to social responsibility. I say characteristic rather than distinctive, since both the roots and the fruits are common to all Christians. But there are certain emphases and connections that are characteristic and constant. So let me take again three representative areas of the living growth of the church – doctrine, liturgy and structure.

i. Doctrine

Here above all Anglicans have nothing exclusive of their own. Their reformation was not born out of some distinctive doctrinal thrust such as that which marked Luther's stress on justification by faith alone or Calvin's on divine predestination or even Wesley's on Christian perfection. Yet if there has been one root which has fed the Anglican stock, and produced its characteristic fruits in the field of social responsibility, it is surely the doctrine of the Incarnation – not of course, as Stephen Sykes has rightly pointed out, that there are any grounds in the basic documents of the Anglican reformation by which the doctrine of the Incarnation may be regarded as more central, say, than that of the Cross. Nevertheless Anglican theology has been dominantly and persistently incarnational, particularly in the nineteenth and twentieth centuries. This was fastened on by the too-little known book brought out in 1953 by the American Calvinist Lewis Smedes, *The Incarnation: Trends in Modern Anglican Thought*, as by Michael Ramsay's masterly survey *From Gore to Temple* (which incidentally failed to notice it). The latter title was seen on my desk by my young son at the time, who thought it described the story of man from barbarism to civilization! There is a sequel by the American Episcopalian Robert J. Page, *New Directions in Anglican Theology*, with the sub-title *From Temple to Robinson*, which it may be surmised is the history of its decline and fall. Actually it is a perceptive survey of the quarter-century from 1939 to 1964, which already now appears a distant scene.

By the Incarnation I have in mind here the basic stress on the Word made *flesh*. For the Word was not simply made word, let alone words. I remember setting the cat among the pigeons at a Lutheran gathering in Germany by saying that to my ears we heard far too much of the 'Wort Gottes': everything seemed to be settled (in this case secular problems of journalism and the press) by what 'the Word of God' *said*. The expostulation that followed had to be heard to be believed!

But the Anglican emphasis has been on the fact that the Word was made matter – and above all man. 'The communication of truth through personality' was Bishop Phillips Brooks's description of preaching, grounded in the event of Christmas celebrated in his matchless hymn 'O little town of Bethlehem'. 'The enmanment of God' is the phrase used by Norman Pittenger, whose major work *The Word Incarnate* remains, I think, a much underrated contribution to Christology, and typically Anglican. From the beginning Ignatius fastened on the distinctive feature of the Christian revelation, which Augustine did not find in the writings of the Platonists nor would have in those of the Hindus or Buddhists, by saying that God was revealed '*anthrōpinōs*', human-wise. Note incidentally that it is as man, *anthrōpos*, not male, *anēr*, that he was revealed. Obviously *Jesus* had to be masculine or feminine, as he had to be black or white (and he wasn't particularly white). But in *Christ* there is neither male nor female, black nor white. The attempt of late (and it really is new doctrine) to use the maleness of Christ (now that the maleness of God has proved something of a broken reed!) as the foundation of an all-male priesthood, so far from being the heart of catholic orthodoxy is surely plain heresy. For the word used of Christ in the creeds and classic formularies is always *anthrōpos*, not *anēr*. But there is no need to institute proceedings: it must soon fall away as a historical curiosity.

The fact that God was made man, and *not* a white man or a black man, was the very simple but utterly basic conviction upon which Trevor Huddleston rested his whole opposition to *apartheid*. And this was and is dynamite – if you follow it through. It was what took Jim Pike on the road to Selma with Martin Luther King. And it accounts for the fact that, despite its 'establishment' image, the Anglican church both in South Africa and in the United States has been in the van of the fight for racial justice (at least many of its bishops and clergy have – the laity have often discovered they had more economic stake in the *status quo*). But this link between incarnational theology and social involvement runs right back in Anglican tradition, through Temple and Scott Holland to Westcott, Gore and Maurice. And one of its characteristics has been to see the church, the body of Christ, as 'the extension of the Incarnation' filling up in its flesh his sufferings and completing his fullness, the pledge and instrument of the redemption of all humanity in the *totus Christus*. It is a doctrine of the church which refuses to isolate it from the redemption of the whole human race, and indeed of nature and the cosmos. Maurice's theology was in this respect I think more truly Anglican, and more biblical, than, say, Pusey's, who bought a high doctrine of the church and its ministry at the expense of a low doctrine of the state. A formula which I hit on very early and which has served me well is this: Have as high a doctrine of the ministry as you like, as long as your doctrine of the church is higher; and have as high a doctrine of the church as you like, as long as your doctrine of the kingdom is higher. For ultimately everything has to be subordinated to the priority of the kingdom of God and his righteousness. That is the proportion of the faith in its fullness, and it means that there can be no gospel at all which is not a social gospel.

ii. Liturgy

Not only is 'the body of Christ' a crucial link between the corporal and the corporate, incarnation and church, but it is the link also between the church and the eucharist. And there is a direct causal relationship between them. For despite the Authorized Version, with its scarcely intelligible (when you come to analyse it) 'We are one bread, one body', it is '*because* of the one bread that we who are many are one body; for we all partake of the one bread' (I Cor. 10.17). It is the eucharist that constantly recreates the church. Again, despite the Authorized Version's 'not discerning the Lord's body', which has focused attention on disrespect to the eucharistic elements, it is, in Moffatt's rendering, if you have no 'sense of the Body', if, that is, you go on behaving, like the Corinthians, individualistically and schismatically, that you cannot but eat condemnation to yourselves (I Cor. 11.29). For in the eucharist you take to yourselves in judgment the one new man in Christ Jesus which your conduct denies. You cannot have Christ without your brother in Christ.

Making the eucharist central, as the Anglican reformers attempted to do more than any of the others, meant making society central. And the restoration of the common cup, as opposed to Romanism that denied it to the laity and to fissiparous Protestantism that divided it into individual tots (I often wonder what that Anglican high churchman John Wesley would have made of that in Methodism!), was much more than a piece of ritual: it was a sacramental sign, an acted parable in the prophetic tradition. The corporate character of the eucharist, despite the Victorian individualism of the 'Anglican eight o'clock', has never been lost sight of. And in recent years of course it has been powerfully reasserted in the Parish Communion. Gregory Dix's article in the symposium of that name presents the theological heart of the revolution, as well as a summary thesis of his brilliant and often beautiful book *The Shape of the*

Liturgy. There is an intimate connection between baptism and the eucharist and the entire shape and style of the *plebs sancta dei*, the holy common people of God. Lionel Thornton's book *The Common Life in the Body of Christ* was another typically 'Anglican' title. But in case the relation between communion and community should be limited to the Christian community (and this would be quite unbiblical: *koinonia* is never used of *a* community), there is the title of a book whose influence was more seminal still, Gabriel Hebert's *Liturgy and Society* – and it is interesting that all three were by monks, who are often regarded as cut off from society. For 'the common life' *is* common life 'in Christ'. The holy communion is the making holy of the common. Henceforth, because again of the Incarnation, we may call nothing common or unclean. I remember once as a green young curate the stunned silence when I threw into a sermon in a Methodist church: 'The more evil you think alcohol is the more reason why you should use it for communion, for this is where it is redeemed.' And as a green young bishop I was never forgiven for saying at the *Lady Chatterley* trial that D. H. Lawrence saw sex as an act of holy communion: 'in the lower case' I added, as I thought, for the professionals of the press – but in vain!

Many years before that I had said in some lectures in America on 'Matter, Power and Liturgy' (included in *On Being the Church in the World*): 'Just as this eucharistic action is the pattern of all Christian action, the sharing of this bread the sign for the sharing of all bread, so this fellowship is the germ of all society renewed in Christ.' Matter (bread and wine), social action ('do this' – in the plural), form the heart of what lies at the centre of the distinctively Christian presence in the world – and that not simply of the church but of the kingdom. For every eucharist is an anticipation of eating and drinking new in the kingdom of God, of the resurrection of the body of all creation. It was William Temple again who spoke of Christianity as 'the most avowedly materialist of all the world's religions' and concluded the *summa* of his philosophy of life in *Nature, Man and God* with a chapter on 'the sacramental universe'. *Everything* is sacramental. This is also of course the emphasis of the Quakers, with whom I have immense sympathy. Indeed if one had the time to be both a Quaker and an Anglican I gladly would, because I could not simply be content with them to celebrate this emphasis by the anomaly of refusing to have sacraments. But all they want to say of the connection between this table and all other tables, this bread and all other bread, this house of God and all other houses of God, I willingly buy. Indeed perhaps the most influential article I ever wrote, in terms of its consequences for the face of the Church of England, was on 'The House Church and the Parish Church' (also in that first collection of essays). It was also, believe it or not now, about the most controversial. It got me nearer losing a job (and that on the staff of a theological college!) than either *Lady Chatterley's Lover* or *Honest to God*. For the idea that you could actually have *holy* communion round the kitchen table, if necessary out of ordinary crockery, was plain desecration – and the resistance to the house communion came much more strongly from the laity than the clergy (unlike that to *Honest to God*) – until, that is, they actually experienced it. It revealed, after all these centuries, a Levitical rather than Christian understanding of the holy, as the opposite of what was common or unclean. Spelt out in liturgy, such is the difference that the Incarnation makes.

iii. Structure

The roots of the Anglican ethos are here almost literally in the soil. Just as there was an intimate connection – and still is – for Israel betwen the people and the land, so Anglicanism has a 'born' relationship to nature and the nation (again these two come from the same root). It was of course part of general Reformation doctrine that *cuius regio eius religio*. Region and religion were intimately linked, and this was a feature of the rise of nationalism in the sixteenth century which Henry VIII was happy to exploit. But that was to make an 'ism' out of, and to distort, something that went far deeper, the rootedness (as in Jesus's parables) of the supernatural in the natural. And this is a characteristic of English theology which goes back well behind the Reformation. Julian of Norwich, for instance, in the fourteenth century (whom I shall be looking at later) sees the supernatural as that which is supremely, superly, natural. The *ecclesia Anglicana*, perhaps because of its rooting in England's green and pleasant island, has been more inextricably bound up both with nature (and where else could the harvest festival have been born?) and the nation than anything distinctively Continental. Despite all discouragement from holocausts and philosophies (whether empirical or linguistic), it has stuck adhesively to natural theology, and its reaction to crisis is not with the Continentals to abandon it but, in the characteristic title of Howard Root's opening essay in *Soundings*, to 'begin all over again'. In fact I remember shocking the Swiss, even more perhaps than the Germans with my observations on 'the Word of God', by saying on the spur of the moment, in

Geneva of all places, that 'all theology is natural theology'. By which I did not mean 'natural' as opposed to 'revealed' theology – St Paul makes it absolutely plain that what the Gentiles know of God through the things he has made is not by unaided human reason but because 'he has revealed it to them' (Rom. 1.19). I meant that all theology, all '*logos*' about '*theos*', which Tillich once defined as 'taking rational trouble about a mystery', starts from where we are. And the Anglican catechism epitomizes this in its first question, which is not about God or Christ or even 'the chief end of man', but simply, 'What is your name?' This is not to reduce theology to anthropology. It is to start from the image of God, which, like the Quakers again or the Cambridge Platonists, Anglican theology has resolutely refused to believe has been totally effaced (if it were, we should never know it). It is to plead, as my father put it, again following Maurice, for 'a theology which starts from the sun and not the clouds, and sees evil from the side of good, and not light in terms of evil'. And with our overcast skies that surely cannot be said to represent a peculiarly English bias! In fact it is where Jesus himself started, who appealed to the God who makes his sun to rise on the evil and the good (Matt. 5.45) and said that if you, 'bad as you are [and he knew what was in man], know how to give your children what is good for them, how much more will your heavenly Father?' (Matt. 7.11; Luke 11.13).

As this inexpungeable link with nature has prevented Anglicanism at its best from being too churchy, so its rooting in the nation has guarded it against being sectarian. Of the two categories into which Troelsch divided religious groups, the 'church-type' and the 'sect-type', there has never been any doubt on which side of the line the Anglican has stood. The whole idea of the national church, with the parson as priest to the parish, not the congregation, goes back far and deep, well beyond the theory of the establishment that was invented to justify and explain it – that church and state, Parliament and Convocation, were but two sides of the same coin. That never corresponded with reality, but it expressed an ideal. And it is an ideal to which Alex Vidler was to resonate as recently again as *Soundings*, that Cambridge Anglican symposium of 1962, citing Arnold, Coleridge and Maurice. 'The Church of England', he said, 'still has the framework of a national church, as distinguished from that of a gathered church, a sect or a religious denomination. . . . It has always aspired to be the church of the whole English people, "whether they will hear or whether they will forbear" '.

This is very different from a 'state church', which our enemies may think of us as, but which we have never sensed ourselves to be. I have not forgotten the culture-shock when first I heard the suffrage from the American Prayer Book (now happily revised), phrased with careful ambiguity to include your local Congressman as well as the federal President, 'O Lord, save the state.' The state church is much more of a German concept, corresponding to the Lutheran polarization of 'throne' and 'altar' which we have never known. The coronation service incidentally – with its roots far back behind the Reformation – encapsulates much Anglican theology. So ironically does the happy arrangement by which the Queen when in Scotland is a Presbyterian. This is sheer nonsense to any denominationalism, but reflects what as an Anglican I feel quite deeply, that wherever I am permanently I should belong to the church of the land, if in Scotland to the Presbyterian, if in France to the Roman Catholic, if in Germany to the Lutheran, if in Roumania to the Orthodox, and so on – though I may still thank God that I don't actually have to live in any of them! In fact I would prefer the Scottish to the English *form* of establishment, but would defend it as a norm not for Erastian reasons (that represents state dominance of the church), but for the reason that Tillich, perhaps surprisingly, defended it (but he remained essentially a European not an American). This is because it reflects the public acknowledgment of the faith by the nation, and not least because it keeps the church open to the nation. It also reflects the fact (not lightly to be thrown away) that the nation deliberately affords a place to the prophet in its midst. We tend to assume that prophets can prophesy only if they are in the wilderness. Yet what Nathan said to David and what Isaiah and Jeremiah said to their people depended upon their standing within the establishment and upon their access to the places of power: they spoke the Word of the Lord from inside rather than outside – even if it resulted, as it did for Jeremiah, in their being thrown out.

None of this of course depends upon the *legal* establishment of the church, which is but the external shell peculiar to the Provinces of Canterbury and York and must be modified (as gradually but decisively it has been in recent years). Yet the position from which one speaks is vital to what is heard – and these days to what is carried. Years ago – and it is many times truer now – Winston Churchill remarked that the order of importance was (*a*) who you were, (*b*) how you said it, and (*c*) what you said. And who you are is greatly determined by the hat you wear – as I discovered with dramatic effect when I became a bishop. I thought I was saying much the same as I had always said, but suddenly everybody took notice. I might be the most junior suffragan in the land, but the world does not observe such niceties. A bishop is a bishop is a bishop, especially when he happens to be in London within local phone call of the media and even more when what he says supposedly contradicts the role in which he says it. Our theology of the world in which God chooses in each generation to become incarnate must take in these non-theological factors.

There are two further corollaries of this link with nature and the nation which I would mention briefly before passing on. First, it has delivered England from what one gets on the continent of Europe: Christian political parties. The assumption has been, and I think it is a healthy one, that Christians should be spread between all the parties and that the Christian witness may not be identified with any one of them. And the idea of the church telling people how to vote, as the Pope used to tell his nuns in Rome how to vote, simply stands our hair on end.

Secondly, whatever notion of 'headship' is to be deduced from this applies to the whole order of creation. The idea, mooted this time among evangelicals, that because St Paul said that the head of the woman is man therefore you cannot have women priests, let alone bishops, must apply equally to prime ministers and queens. To confine it to the spiritual and the ecclesiastical is a very spiky thing to do. Rather, the obligation of Christians is to expose *all* notions of natural headship or lordship – political, economic, sexual – to the searching examination of the gospel, as was done, belatedly, and that under evangelical leadership, in the case of slavery and is now being done, slowly, in the case of women. (Following the judiciary and the Stock Exchange, the Jockey Club and the Kennel Club have now admitted women in England. The House of Clergy of the General Synod may be expected to follow suit any decade.)

So far I have simply been describing the rootedness of the Anglican ethos, through its dominant concern for incarnation, in the texture of doctrine, liturgy and structure. This does not of itself say anything about how one expresses and exercises such involvement. That can be profoundly conservative or profoundly radical. The links I have traced are in fact with highly conservative things – and what more than liturgy or the land? Yet the effect is reactionary only if, one-sidedly, institution is set over against event, priest against prophet, Catholic substance (to use Tillich's distinction) against Protestant principle. But this is precisely what, when truest to itself, the Anglican settlement has refused to do. It may have been the Conservative party at prayer, but only when it has slumbered and prophecy has been silent. At their best and most outward-looking all its constituent parties have found themselves on the frontiers of social change.

This hardly needs stressing with regard to the Anglo-Catholics (though their constant temptation has been to become church- rather than kingdom-orientated), nor with the broad churchmen (though their danger is to become latitudinarian and woolly); but a word perhaps is in place with regard to the evangelicals. No one could accuse a Simeon or Wilberforce or a Charles Raven or David Sheppard in our day of simply being concerned with disembodied souls. But modern conservative and even liberal evangelicalism seems to have lost its way. We are all familiar with the pietists, fundamentalists, charismatics and the rest who think it theologically wicked to get involved with politics. But it is not only they, but the profoundly untheological do-nothingers, who latch on when they hear a man like Edward Norman attacking the politicization of the churches in a manner which appears to be apolitical, but is in fact strongly to the right. This is the equivalent in English political terms of the dockers rooting for Enoch Powell on race, and it is an unhealthy sign. But let me presume to advert also to the stance of the more liberal evangelicals, who should know better. Here it seems to me a case of innocents abroad who because of a one-sided emphasis on the Atonement rather than the Incarnation have little doctrine of the world – of flesh, matter and power – and therefore little understanding of politics. In the classic words of Roger Fulford on Queen Victoria's uncle, the Duke of Cambridge, 'Like all those who do not understand politics he drifted imperceptibly to the right.' With neither a theological nor a political critique that cuts at all deeply, they substitute moralizing. And this is actually made into a virtue by Moral Re-armament which, in effect though not in intention, is one of the most reactionary forces around today, both morally and politically. (My last contact with them was when they brought Ian Smith's son to see me, a nice lad who had read theology at Salisbury, as a great white hope along with Bishop Muzorewa in Rhodesia!)

Yet, properly understood, there is not a negative antithesis between the conservative and the radical, the priestly and the prophetic, but a positive polarity. Indeed in our day who are more radical than the conservationists, who are concerned with preserving the most elemental things in our life-style? And without making conservation too into an 'ism' I have every sympathy with them –

though it is interesting how the radical non-violence, say, of the Friends of the Earth, for all its pacific nature, sends shivers down the spine of the law and order lobby, the self-proclaimed guardians of institutionalized violence.

Since my title is 'the roots of a radical', let me close by saying how I would view the true relation between roots and fruits, by giving some examples of the priority, as I see it, of centres over edges. I am *not* saying that this is how all should see it. Indeed the joy and the pain of Anglicanism, unlike the Romanism even of Vatican II which, as Stephen Sykes has pointed out, entirely failed to prepare the church to expect, let alone to embrace, the conflict it provoked, comes precisely from welcoming the creative tension of many viewpoints. For it really does believe not in a unitary and hierarchical model of truth and authority but in a diffused and pluriform one.

Here is a check list. When I counted them there happened to be ten, but one could go on indefinitely, and they are not a new 'ten propositions', let alone ten commandments.

1. Integrity is more fundamental than orthodoxy. A man of unimpeachable orthodoxy but uncertain integrity is a far greater threat to Christian truth than the man of questionable orthodoxy but undeniable integrity. Moreover, the man who however mistakenly or inadequately (and 'way-outs' and reactionaries can be equally embarrassing) genuinely intends what the church means is unlikely in the long run to damage it seriously – for others can supply the correctives. If he holds to the centre he will be all right, however unreliable an ally on the edges. For the radical who sets integrity above orthodoxy will always be a bad party man, politically and ecclesiastically: he cannot be guaranteed to follow the party line, because lines do not determine his priorities. Those who believe that truth consists in toeing the line, or the defence of orthoxody in bringing theologians into line, cannot understand this. It is still perhaps the greatest gulf between the Papalist ethos and the Anglican.

2. Love has priority over law. This does not mean that the radical does not care about law. On the contrary, one of the frontiers on which I have been most engaged is law-reform – capital punishment, censorship, suicide, abortion, homosexuality, and sexual legislation generally. And what is his fundamental concern in this field? The primary function of law in society is not to prohibit but to protect, not to enforce morals but to safeguard persons, their privacies and their freedoms; and where there is no need for pro-

tection it should not intervene. Its aim should be to maximize the area of freedom and moral responsibility, and then to have good and enforceable ring-fences to protect persons against exploitation – set as far from the centre as possible. But I will say no more on this here since I have expanded on it at length in chapter VI.

3. Persons have priority over principles. This again is so obvious in the teaching of Jesus that one would think it needed no saying. 'The sabbath was made for the sake of man and not man for the sabbath' (Mark 2.27). As Paul Ramsey well put it in his *Basic Christian Ethics*, 'A faithful Jew stayed as close as possible to the observance of the law even when he had to depart from it. Jesus stayed as close as possible to the fulfilment of human need, no matter how wide of the . . . law this led him.' I think I need hardly say more except to admit that this of course is an exceedingly dangerous priority. The saying I have just quoted follows the question, 'Have you never read what David did?' And he actually ate the shew-bread – and fed it to his gang – to satisfy human hunger (Mark 2.25f)! Yet Jesus used this example, as a true radical, not to abolish the sabbath (like a revolutionary) nor to tinker with it (like a reformist) but to go to its roots, to ask what it is *for*, how it can really serve, and preserve, persons. Of course you can use this freedom, as St Peter says, as a cloak for totally unprincipled or individualistic action (I Peter 2.16) – and that is no expression of love. But to reverse the priority and exalt principles over persons, as code-morality does, is in the long run more deadly both to the church and the world.

4. It is more deadly because it denies, fourthly, the priority of relationships, of breathing, feeling, experienced, existential realities over any abstractions from them. When I asked what it would be useful to talk on in these lectures the first heading of the reply began: 'We need a theology of the experience of human love. Maoridom apart, New Zealand is a society (on the surface) which doesn't know what to do with its emotions (except in sport).' In this it seems rather parallel to what one saw in white (as opposed to black) South Africa, and is very much borne out by the analysis of the New Zealand character by that marvelllously free and radical Roman Catholic priest Felix Donelly, entitled significantly *Big Boys Don't Cry*. But in this concern for a theology which starts from the flesh let me simply here recommend two books which I had occasion to quote before. The first is by the Brazilian Christian Rubem Alves, who in conscious contrast with Jürgen Moltmann's title *The Theology of Hope*, called his *A Theology of Human Hope*. Like the Church

Catechism he began from the *humanum*, the humanity of God, with the actual agonizing yearnings of hope and liberation which God has stirred to life in the breasts of his creatures especially in Latin America, and he does his theology of the kingdom from there in terms of what it means 'to make and to keep life human'. The other is Charles Davis's book, called significantly *Body as Spirit*, and subtitled 'the place of feeling in religion'. It is not easy reading, but it has some perceptive things to say on the gut issues of life and death, sex and evil. This is where incarnational theology has got in my judgment to start – with relationships; and the work of Harry Williams and of Rosemary Haughton, in her books *On Trying to be Human* and *The Transformation of Man*, provide other examples of it.

5. The priority of stands over standards. 'Standards don't change', an advertisement for the *Daily Telegraph* has recently been assuring us in England. But unfortunately they do, constantly. 'New occasions teach new duties: time makes ancient good uncouth.' If you invest your concern for stability in the *content* of the moral commands you will find you are continually being threatened by change; and you will dig in behind that rampart of all good men and true, 'the *Daily Telegraph* mind'. Moreover, despite Moral Rearmament, you can't have more than one absolute (finally you've got to decide when and where to give priority, say, to lying over killing). The only absolute for the Christian is love, and on *that* you have got to be prepared to take *unconditional* stands and say, 'Here I stand, I can no other.' What these will be will vary from time to time, issue to issue, person to person. But this is how standards, the second-order generalizations, are discerned, related and revised. The prophet is the person, however humble, who helps us to see what are the sticking-points, and what the stretching-points, in our attitudes to the world at any given time or place.

6. The priority of justice over order. Order is an immensely important value in the preservation of persons: it can scarcely be overestimated, especially in an increasingly violent society. But it *can* be overestimated. Justice is more basic than order – which so often turns out to set a greater premium on property than persons. And one has got to ask *why* we live in an increasingly violent society. Writ large one can see it again in South Africa, where the stickers one saw around Wits University said it succinctly: 'Less laws, more justice'. As Dom Helder Camara, the Archbishop of Recife in North-East Brazil, has shown (and as I shall be expanding in chapter 7), 'the spiral of violence' begins with the violence of oppression, the institutionalized violence of the unfair society, before it provokes

the grim cycle of the violence of protest and the violence of repression. *Merely* to tighten up the last, however necessary, say, in retaining the presence of the army in Ulster, *solves* nothing.

7. The priority of *ethos* over ethics. That we need ethics, a relevant and coherent network of conduct which commands the maximum consensus, no sane person would deny. We similarly need a system of criminal law, a polity and an economic order which measure up to the same criteria. But it was not the mission of Jesus to supply any of these, not even an ethic. There is not *a* Christian ethic – though it is the continual duty of Christians as responsible members of their particular society to work away at all these networks and keep them in repair. But there is a Christian 'ethos', which the dictionary defines as 'characteristic spirit, settled character' – though its embodiments and manifestations will be as diverse as the culture it informs and the lump it leavens. Perhaps the distinction I have in mind can be pointed up by the difference between the invitation to communion in the Book of Common Prayer to 'those who are in love and charity with their neighbours and intend to lead a new life' and the minute revision which some slipped in, to those who 'intend to lead *the* new life'. No one is decrying the need to live a new life – which will vary with every individual. But the basis of that, and the basis of receiving communion together, is *the* new life – just as the New English Bible correctly in my judgment renders Phil. 2.5 not as 'Have this mind in you which *was* also in Christ Jesus' – as if it is a matter of copying a way of life, even that of the Master – but 'Let your bearing towards one another arise out of your life in Christ Jesus', out of the great new reality of your being 'in Christ'. The ethic flows from the ethos.

8. The priority of function over form. As in art, form follows function. All forms are secondary, yet are organically essential to proper functioning. Hence they can distort function. Notoriously is this the case, say, in the relation of architecture to liturgy: the building speaks louder than anything we do or say in it – and so much church building has started from form (what a church 'ought' to look like) or like the Gothic-revivalists from the shells created and sanctified by quite a different, medieval form of life. But there are other still more insidiously dangerous structures. The point was made some years ago in the World Council of Churches' discussion on 'The Missionary Structure of the Congregation' that heretical structures are today more distortive and destructive of the mission and ministry of the church than most conceptual heresies. And these are propagated and perpetuated by the most conservative

rather than by the most radical. There is a parallel too in the doctrinal field to the effect of structural fundamentalism in the ecclesiastical. I would illustrate this again from the key doctrine of the Incarnation. The complete and utter genuineness of Christ's humanity is agreed by all to be a *sine qua non* of anything further we may wish to say about him. Yet it is hardly open to question that it is the most traditionally 'orthodox' statements of the sinless perfection of Christ's manhood that give modern post-Darwinian, post-Freudian man greatest cause to doubt whether Jesus's was a genuinely human existence, let alone a uniquely human existence. It is those who are *not* taking the risks of exploration and reformulation who may find themselves paradoxically in greater peril of encouraging heresy.

9. From this follows the priority of organism over organization. Again let no one decry the need for organization. If we are to do battle against the principalities and powers we need good organization, efficient structures, and lines of communication and accountability that work. I was not a working bishop for ten years without learning how crucial that is. Yet the organic always has priority over the organizational. I have often said that radical and fundamenalist are but two names for the same basic concern. Yet it is no accident that the one uses an organic, the other an inorganic, metaphor. The effect of digging round roots and of digging round foundations can be very different. And when fruits decay they release seeds; when buildings decay they produce urban blight – or leave white elephants – whether in the church or in the world.

10. That brings me finally to the priority which really underlies all the rest, of existence over essence. When Kierkegaard was asked to define what he meant by the 'existential' he told a story, of the man who built a castle – and lived in a shack nearby. The radical is a person who lives by his or her roots and this means getting stuck in, taking sides, coming off the fence. The Anglican *via media* does not mean occupying, in Maurice's phrase, 'an invisible equatorial line between Romanism and Protestantism', still less treading the Irishman's 'narrow path between good and evil'. It is not being neutral between justice and injustice or between rich and poor. There is a built-in bias in the gospel, and the report *Theological Freedom and Social Responsibility* uses the phrase, as a criterion, interestingly, of *liturgical* revival, 'the passionate participation of the church with the world's pain'. That is the edge of engagement to which the centre must constantly push us. Otherwise all the canvassed concern in Anglican circles for clearer definition, for tighter

discipline, for better ring-fences (none of them to be despised) will merely enclose a hollow – and we shall be left a sounding brass and a tinkling Canterbury bell.

III

HONEST TO CHRIST TODAY

As one seeks to follow the continuing debate on Christology, holding to the centre while pushing out at the edges, I would fasten on four points at which, it would seem to me, honesty is particularly required today to the truth as it is in Jesus. By honesty I mean complete openness to the truth in whatever aspect, wherever it may lead; and of these four the first two are what I would call sticking-points, the second two stretching-points.

i. Honesty to the irreducibility of incarnation

The Myth of God Incarnate edited by John Hick started with an essay by Maurice Wiles called 'Christianity without Incarnation?'. No doubt, like the over-all title, it was intended to be provocative, but the effect has been to produce more heat than light. It is like commending 'Christianity without the Bible' when you mean 'Christianity without biblicism'. You can explain that what you are questioning is a particular way of stating God's relation to Christ, but the explanation will not be heard. It will be assumed that you are denying the reality that the statement is about. Perhaps indeed that is the case, but this can only be decided by a careful disentangling of the issues, and by listening hard and long to what is being said on each side.

When the rushed riposte came out, *The Truth of God Incarnate* edited by Michael Green, I found it difficult to decide which was the worse book. On reflection I think this dubious honour must surely be accorded to the reply. Undoubtedly it scored some palpable hits, exposing confusions and superficialities in the original essayists, not least in their treatment of the New Testament. Yet the best thing in it, the review of the first book by John Macquarrie, could equally have been turned against much in the collection in which he allowed it to appear. 'It is surely inexcusable', he wrote, 'that in a serious work the key term "myth" should be introduced for the first time in its loosest possible sense.' But the second book does exactly the same, and its very title fell straight into the trap of opposing 'truth' to 'myth' and thus abetting the popular understanding of myth as fiction rather than a profound form of truth. But above all it failed to listen seriously to the important questions being raised, however 'reassuring' its answers, and it is not surprising that it should have been brushed aside with scarcely a mention in the third round, *Incarnation and Myth: The Debate Continued*, edited by Michael Goulder.

I do not intend to comment in detail on this further round, which is conducted at a considerably more sophisticated level and contains some real clarification. As one who has been a member of neither team, I would simply reflect from the side-lines on an encounter in which both sides seem so often to be going past each other without meeting. I find myself wanting to affirm what each is saying without being committed to what the other is denying. In other words, I believe there is a polarization going on which in my judgment falsifies the truth.

But let me first say positively why I want to hold to the irreducibility of incarnation as a distinctive, perhaps the distinctive, Christian category, while at the same time sitting loose to many ways of stating it which have come to be associated with traditional orthodoxy.

Let us start with a statement of scripture which all, I take it, would accept as central and yet which remarkably is not cited in the entire debate. It is St Paul's assertion in II Cor. 5.19, that 'God was in Christ reconciling the world to himself'. This seems to me to present the heart of the distinctive message of the New Testament: the identification of God with the action of Christ and of Christ with the action of God, and that not just at any point but at the climax and turning-point of salvation history. But it is notable also for what it does not say. It does not say that God was Christ nor in any simplistic sense that Christ was God, but that he represents the definitive act of God, that he is God about his decisive work. What he does God does, so that Christ is not just a man doing human things divinely, like any saint or seer, but a man doing divine things humanly. To be met by him is to be met by

God: he stands *in loco dei*, as his personal representative, so that men's attitude to him determines God's attitude to them. In terms of the parable of Mark 12.1–12, he is the son, one who is just as human as the servants but who stands in quite a different relationship to the owner of the vineyard. And this is the inescapable presupposition of the whole synoptic picture. The 'I' with which he speaks and acts, without so much as a 'Thus saith the Lord' is 'with authority', 'from source', with the '*amen*' of God himself. This is what St John draws out by setting on Jesus' lips the statement that 'he who has seen me has seen the Father' (John 14.9) or the claim, already presupposed in the tradition behind Matthew and Luke (Matt. 11.27; Luke 10.22), that everything the Father has is his, because everything he has is the Father's. (This does not mean, to use a distinction to which I shall return in the first of my stretching-points, that he is *totum dei*, everything there is of God, but that he is *totus deus*, God through and through: everything about him bespeaks God.) There is not an identity of person between him and the Father – he is wholly subordinate to him as to one greater than himself, indeed than all. But because he lives in a relationship of utter filial obedience and is totally one with him, he is, in John's analogy, the 'spit an' image' of God, 'as of an only son of his father' (1.14; there are no articles in the Greek). He is what the writer to the Hebrews calls 'the reflection of his glory, the stamp of his very being' (1.3), or Paul 'the son of his love', 'the image of the invisible God' (Col. 1.13,15), or John again 'the Word' (1.1–18), the very embodiment in flesh and blood of 'the self-expressive activity of God' (to use Pittenger's paraphrase). He is not God (*ho theos*), nor simply divine (*theios*), but *theos*, which the NEB gets, I think, fairly precisely by 'What God was, the Word was' (1.1). There is an equivalence, a 1:1 relationship, an identity of value and function, which is reflected throughout the New Testament in the interchangeability of God-language and Christ-language (and for that matter Spirit-language) *without* simply identifying or equating them.

It is this conviction that is affirmed or 'pegged' by the assertion of the *incarnation*, not indeed of God *simpliciter*, as if Jesus were God dressed up and walking this earth, but of the Word, of God's creative, self-expressive activity from the beginning, fully and finally embodied in *this man*, who is completely and utterly a man like the rest of us, in origin, nature and destiny. As the author to the Hebrews insists, he is and must be 'taken from among men' (5.1), 'of one stock' with 'those whom he consecrates' (2.11). He is not more than a man, with something extra that the others haven't got, but the man in whom God perfectly comes through, the human agent in all his freedom responding, as process theology puts it, to the 'aim' and 'lure' of the divine love. He lives God, because God lives him. He is God expressed or given exegesis (John 1.18), as Ignatius was to put it, *anthrōpinōs*, humanly, or, in Theodore of Mopsuestia's phrase, 'as in a son'. If one wanted to get away from the *word* 'incarnation' (and it *could* suggest the mere coating in flesh of a divine Being), then I would propose the phrase of the Taiwanese theologian Choan Seng Song (under the inspiration of Barth's 'humanity of God'), 'the humanization of God', which has the advantage of linking it to the on-going divine mission of humanization committed to the church. But nothing less than this I think is faithful to the New Testament witness as a whole, which I believe to be remarkably consistent, through the synoptists, John, Paul and the Epistle to the Hebrews – however much, as Browning put it of the Fourth Gospel, what first were guessed as 'points' became known as 'stars', as the relationship to God lived out by Jesus primarily in terms of verbs and adverbs was made explicit in titles of glory.

Having said this, however, as strongly as I can, I want to go on to dissociate this traditional and I believe entirely orthodox statement from other positions which in the course of history have been identified with it and from which those who want Christianity 'without incarnation' are correct in wishing to distance themselves.

The first is the tendency to turn the Incarnation into an event different in kind and discrete from every other revelation or act of God, so that it becomes, in Whitehead's language, the anomalous exception rather than the chief exemplification. The prologue to the Fourth Gospel, the *locus classicus* for incarnational theology, is clearly against any such isolation – as is Matthew's Emmanuel, 'God with us' (1.22f.), which is but the climax and fulfilment of all to which Hebrew religion pointed (Isa. 7.14). For the light that comes to focus in Jesus is the light that enlightens *every* man and the process which ends in the embodiment of the Logos in a person is but the climax of what begins in nature and history and a people. There is indeed a distinctness, a uniqueness of status, which leads John to reserve the term 'son' for Jesus while calling Christians 'children of God' and Paul to speak of Christians as sons only by adoption. Yet to balance the description of Jesus, as earlier of Israel, as the 'only' son (*monogenēs*) (John 1.14,18), which like its synonym 'beloved' (*agapētos*) implies in biblical usage specialness rather than exclusiveness, the New Testament speaks of him also as the 'first-born' of a large family of brothers (Rom. 8.29; Heb. 1.6), the eldest of 'many sons' (Heb. 2.10). The two designations may logically be incompatible but together they express a difference which is never simply one of kind, though he has an unrepeatable role, but also of degree. He is unique not because he is abnormal but because he alone is the truly normal man, *the* son of Adam and son of God which the rest of us are called but, except through him, fail to be.

Secondly, though it surely hardly now needs saying, a doctrine of incarnation is in no way tied or committed to a theology of two 'natures', divine and human, through which the God-man was in patristic eyes supposed to operate. This terminology was indeed common both to the Alexandrian and Antiochene schools and is nowhere more vividly illustrated than in the mediating *Tome* of Leo. But no one could today defend the exegesis of scripture which implies that the Christ did some things as God and some things as man, or even everything in 'dual control', and it is so generally abandoned by theologians who cannot possibly be dismissed as reductionist (strongly, for instance, by Pannenberg), that it is surely unnecessary to defend it as part of the orthodox package, however traditional. If today we wish to use such categories, we must say unequivocally that Christ had one nature, a human nature, and one will, a human will, *through* which the nature and will of God are expressed by perfect obedience, though this perfection, as the writer to the Hebrews insists, is achieved only through suffering and struggle. 'I have come, O God, to do *thy* will' is a text he applies to Christ as to every other man (10.5–7); and the gospel evidence is represented not by an internal debate between the human and divine wills of *Christ* but by the agonizing wrestling of one who struggles as a full and fallible human being to pray to his Father, '*Not* my will but *thine* be done'.

But, thirdly and above all, it is not only the language of the two natures that must be detached from a modern doctrine of incarnation but, I believe, the much more damaging notion of *anhypostasia* or *enhypostasia*. This asserts that the 'person' which 'had' the natures is not human but divine, or at most that the human *hypostasis* or personhood of Jesus is somehow included in or constituted by that of God. Christ is thereby viewed as a divine Being who 'took' a human nature as well as his own: 'Veiled in flesh the Godhead see.' It is this doctrine which is currently being questioned (and defended) under the unhappy phrase a 'literal' incarnation, namely, that the person of the incarnate Jesus *is* none other than the second Person of the Trinity living a human life and dying a human death.

And however much a kenotic Christology, stressing the self-emptying of God, may mollify the clashes of the two 'natures' (for instance, in what a truly incarnate Christ could know or do), it cannot do anything to mitigate the problem of how a divine supernatural Being could *be* a totally human historical individual, a genuine product of the evolutionary process like every other member of the species *homo sapiens*. For the kenotic solution presupposes that the subject of the *kenōsis* is the Logos and *not* man, even though it may still contribute valuable insights into how the humiliation of a condemned criminal can nevertheless most truly represent the power of God and the wisdom of God.

The real issue is whether this notion is of the essence of the matter, so that abandoning it means changing the classic doctrine into something that can no longer claim to be a theology of incarnation but, it is said, 'merely' one of inspiration or some form of unitarianism. For if 'underneath' (to use the metaphor of substance) Jesus is not God but 'a man' like everyone else, has not the pass been sold? What distinctive is left?

The first thing to be said is that this theory of *anhypostasia*, or the 'impersonal humanity' of Christ, was not universally accepted, unlike that of the two natures, even in the patristic church. It was vigorously resisted by the Antiochene as opposed to the Alexandrian school (however unsatisfying may have been the former's own formulations) and it is at most implicit in the Definition of Chalcedon. Consequently, as the great Cambridge patristic scholar William Telfer put it, with the silencing of the Antiochene protest 'Chalcedon failed to prevent a modified Apollinarianism from becoming the orthoxody of the Middle Ages'. In modern times the theory has been rejected by many theologians who would not dream of supposing they were abandoning the doctrine of the Incarnation but were trying rather to be true to its real meaning. One could mention, recently, Norman Pittenger, whose classic work is specifically called *The Word Incarnate*; Dietrich Bonhoeffer who termed it in his *Christology* 'the last refuge of docetism'; Piet Schoonenberg who actually received a *nihil obstat* for his book *The Christ*, where he turns the theory on its head and says it was the *Word* that was anhypostatic (i.e. not a person) until it took individuality in the man Jesus; James Mackey, the Roman Catholic successor of T. F. Torrance at Edinburgh, who describes it in his *Jesus: The Man and the Myth* as 'the least possible form of Apollinarianism, or the most tolerable, whichever expression is preferred'; and, finally, Geoffrey Lampe, who in his Bampton Lectures *God as Spirit* claims that 'when Jesus is identified with the pre-existent Son, belief in a true incarnation of God in Jesus is weakened'.

The issue is whether this *theory* of incarnation has any more status or credibility than many a theory of the atonement that has been formulated to present the teaching of scripture. Certainly it safeguards the initiative of God in Christ 'visiting' his people and 'sending' his Son to redeem mankind. And one can understand how the pre-existence language of the Wisdom literature and the New Testament was interpreted to mean that a divine Being, subsequently designated the Second Person of the Trinity, came down from heaven, walked this earth as a man, before returning whence he came. This is a picture-story, or myth, which was to take powerful hold on the Christian imagination. But it is questionable (as I argued in my *Human Face of God*) whether the New Testament writers who use the language of pre-existence, Paul, John and the author to the Hebrews, are really presupposing by it more than the *personification*, already familiar in Hellenistic Judaism, of the Wisdom, Word, Spirit and Son of God as agencies of *his* personal activity – rather than seeing them as self-subsistent divine persons. But whether the transition was made in the New Testament or after it, it was clearly, as Lampe has drawn out, the result of Christians having known Jesus as *a person*, as a real historical individual. To register the conviction that in this man was fulfilled and embodied the meaning of God reaching back to the very beginning, they proclaim him as his Word, his Wisdom, his Image, his Son, from all eternity. In so doing they read back, or retroject, his human personhood as the subject of the divine personification – just as they project it in his heavenly 'post-existence' as a person seated at God's right hand. This is a harmless and indeed a profound myth – as when Paul says of the Old Testament imagery that 'the rock that followed them was Christ' (I Cor.10.4). But in due course the process is reversed and the divine Person becomes the subject of Jesus's *human* experience. Thereby his humanity is rendered questionable, as it never is in the New Testament, even in the Fourth Gospel, which speaks of him as 'a man' twice as often as all the others put together.

The effect of this myth, however vivid a representation of God's being in Jesus, is, when stood on its head and made into a theory to explain the reality of his historical existence, dangerously distortive. As John Knox insisted in his *Humanity and Divinity of Christ*, it makes pre-existence and genuine humanity mutually incompatible *in a way that they never appear to be for the New Testament writers.* This should surely in itself make us wonder whether we are interpreting them right. At any rate it is arguable, I would say probable, that what they are saying is that this *man*, whose origin 'at the human level' (*kata sarka*) from the same stock as the rest of mankind they could not doubt or question, also incarnates and brings to fulfilment 'at the spiritual level' (*kata pneuma*) everything that *God* is and has been doing from the beginning. 'In him', as Paul puts it, 'the complete being of the Godhead came to dwell', and in the *totus Christus* continues to dwell, 'bodily' (Col. 1.19; 2.9). This is I believe as high a doctrine of the Incarnation as one could want – yet without being tied to a way of stating it which in recent years has come to be recognized as more and more questionable. The authors of *The Myth* were entirely right to question it. Where in my judgment they went wrong was to present this as a version of Christianity 'without incarnation' and in so doing to offer an interpretation of the New Testament evidence which is often partial and reductionist.

On the other side, the defenders of traditional orthoxody seem often to be betrayed into making the 'literal' or 'ontological' identity of Christ with God an *articulus vel stantis vel cadentis fidei*, a belief without which saving faith in Christ would be impossible. If, one hears it being said, he was *not* really 'at bottom' a divine Being, the Second Person of the Trinity, and thus different *in kind* from every other man, why should we give our allegiance to him rather than anyone else? But this reasoning is of a piece with the argument of the older apologetics that one must accept Jesus as the Christ *because* he fulfils the Old Testament prophecies, or performs the miracles of the Messiah, or was born of a virgin, or rose physically from the dead. It is to make these things conditions of believing (or earlier 'proofs') of his messiahship rather than *expressions* of this faith set forth by some, but not necessarily by all, of those who would call themselves Christians. The virgin birth, for instance, which is mentioned by only two writers in the New Testament, would generally today be accepted as a corollary rather than a condition of believing in the Incarnation. Similarly, to say that Christ was a being of a different, divine substance from the rest of us (as distinct from saying that in this man the fullness of deity dwelt embodied and was uniquely reflected 'as in a son') is but one way of expressing belief in the Incarnation, and one that neither scripture nor tradition unanimously endorses. To believe in Christ because, and only if, he personally is 'God' reverses the order of faith, which dares to say of this man 'my Lord and my God' (John 20.28), even if, as for the first disciples, there be no 'ontological' or genetic difference between him and any other man. Confession of the divinity of Christ is an existential affirmation that like Thomas one finds oneself in him saved and convicted by God, not a necessary deduction from something physically or metaphysically exceptional in his make-up.

Yet one can still hear the retort that this is not to take his 'divinity' seriously. To the upholders of conservative orthodoxy it seems to be saying that Christ comes from the side of man and *not* from the side of God. But the New Testament forbids any such either-or. It says, to use the terms of the Fourth Gospel (and one can hardly appeal to a higher Christology), that Jesus comes *both* from, or out of, Nazareth *and* from, or out of, the Father. He is the totally human being, of whom at this level the Jews can quite properly say, 'We know where this man comes from' (John 7.27, 41), who is also the expression in all its fullness of the Logos who is *theos* (1.1–18). And, as for Paul and the writer to the Hebrews, he is 'the son' (which means both the expression of God and the response to God) whom God has waited from all eternity to send into the world, the one who perfectly images him. And this divine humanity or sonship is the final cause or entelechy of creation, that which holds within it the aim and goal of the entire process. As in the Jewish wisdom myth (Prov. 8.22–31; etc.), he was with God from the beginning. Through him, on account of him, he, God, created and sustains all the orders of existence, appointing him 'heir' to the whole universe (John 1.1–3; I Cor. 8.6; Col. 1.15–17; Heb. 1.2f). He is the one too in whom the judgment or justification of the world-process is vested – 'because he is son of man' (John 5.27; again there are no articles in the Greek). What Blake called 'the human form divine' is the clue to the meaning of everything. This is a son-shaped universe, a Christic cosmos. Its model, its 'stamp' or character, as the writer to the Hebrews insists (1.13–6), is not angelic but human. And the only one so far (for he is but the firstfruits, the forerunner of the race) perfectly to wear the human form divine, the *morphē theou*, is Jesus. This, I am convinced (with Oscar Cullmann and others), is what Paul means in Phil. 2.6 by his being 'in the form of God' – not that he was 'God by nature' and had to 'become' man, but that he was the true Adam, the archetypal son of God (Luke 3.38). *Morphē* (form), like *eikōn* (image), *homoiōma* (likeness), *charactēr* (stamp) or *doxa* (glory, or rather reflection, as in I Cor. 11.7), is man-language, which characterizes Christ as the perfect self-representation, as opposed to the distorting mirror, of God.

To bring out Paul's meaning I could perhaps close this section with a paraphrase of this classic passage (Phil. 2.6–11), where the deepest, truest significance of Christ, what he really was (*hyparchōn*) at the level of 'spirit', is phrased not in terms of pre-existence so much as in terms of ideal or true existence (as with the Johannine Son of man whose home is always in heaven, whose whole life, that is to say, is lived in God). This I believe to be the meaning also of the closely parallel Pauline passage in II Cor. 8.9, which does not refer simply to a pre-incarnate state but to the wealth of his continuous inner relationship to God: 'You know the grace of our Lord Jesus Christ: he was rich, yet for your sake became poor, so that through his poverty you might become rich.' So here, if we may paraphrase what Paul is saying of Christ:

> God shaped his entire being. He was the perfect reflection of his glory. He might have lived wholly in that unclouded glory. But he did not think being God-like a state to be selfishly enjoyed (or grasped at). Instead he emptied himself of everything. His life took the shape of a slave. He was found living exactly like other men, accepting the common pattern of the human lot. This utterly humble obedience of his led him all the way to death, to a criminal's death at that. This is why God exalted him higher even than he was before (or to the very heights), bestowing upon him the title of his own supremacy, so that at the name of Jesus everything in heaven and earth and the world below should bow the knee and openly confess Jesus Christ as 'Lord' – though always to the glory of God the Father.

This I believe to be an interpretation of the central message of the New Testament which does justice both to the complete humanity of Jesus and to the initiative of God in him for which the distinctive category of incarnation (or some other equivalent) is ultimately indispensable.

ii. Honesty to the Jesus of history as part of the Christ of faith

One of the most distinctive things about the early Christians is that they wrote not simply epistles, apocalypses, manuals of discipline, etc., like the Qumran community, but gospels – tying their message of the Christ of faith to what Jesus himself did and said when he came into Galilee preaching the kingdom of God until the time that he was taken up. The gospels were anything but pure unvarnished history, but they were not pure theology either. They were theological history – proclamations of the meaning of the history really entered into, in all its divine significance and redemptive power. And if the persons and the events they present had not existed or had never happened or had been very different, they would on their own confession have been found liars. If as the result of historical discoveries or historical criticism we were to become convinced that the credibility-gap between the Christ of faith and the Jesus of history was too great, I believe it would make a real difference. In other words I agree with Dodd over against Tillich in the fascinating discussion reported in the appendix to F. W. Dillistone's life of the former, that faith is vulnerable to historical research at this point and that there is no theological insurance policy that can guarantee immunity against the acids of criticism. If it could be shown for instance that Jesus of Nazareth had a police record as long as your arm, or had gone into hiding allowing another to be crucified in his place, or even that he was just another Palestinian freedom-fighter, then frankly there are other candidates. Attempts have been made to deny this vulnerability, by saying that we can never get behind the church's picture of the Christ and do not need to, or that there is little we can say but that it does not matter. Although it may be unfashionable, I would want to contend both for the need of the quest of the historical Jesus and for its real possibility. I increasingly believe that there has been a sort of treason of the clerks at this point – an undue and almost irresponsible scepticism of the wise which has been a good deal less than justified by the sources and which has sold the church short and thrown the believer back into the hands of the fundamentalists. There will never be certainty, only greater and lesser degrees of probability. Yet I refuse to accept, for instance, that we cannot say anything with assurance about the character of Jesus and that Christology consists, as it has been put, in paying him either moral or metaphysical compliments. Nor do I believe that the early Christians had no interest in the historical questions, and I am now persuaded – though this is not the place to pursue it – that with all proper critical responsibility one may return a considerably more certain answer, say, to the chronology of the ministry of Jesus than the fashion of recent scholarship has assumed.

I would want to throw down the challenge as I have in my *Redating the New Testament* to the scientific establishment to look much more closely at the detailed evidence, internal and external, and ask whether there really is justification for postulating a long tunnel-period between the events and the records at the end of which we can have no confidence that the train that comes out laden with ecclesiastical baggage is recognizably the same as the one that went in. I hear the classical scholars, whose books New Testament scholars do not now read any more than they read ours, saying to us, 'You have no idea what good sources you have.' I want to question what I would see as the tyranny of unexamined presuppositions in much of the current post-Bultmannian critical orthodoxy, which I believe will come to be recognized as just as subjective and arbitrary as the Hegelian schema of development which F. C. Baur and his followers imposed on the evolution of the New Testament documents and their theology a century ago. I have no desire to propose a new schema or strait-jacket. I merely want to ask a lot of questions and plead in an old-fashioned way for more self-critical attention to the foundations of New Testament introduction on which so much of the superstructure has been built. This is studied for the most part in students' first year in theology, when they are incapable of doing much more than absorbing and reproducing what the textbooks say. They then go to the more exciting questions of New Testament interpretation and doctrinal construction, and if they are bright they write their Ph.Ds and become professors, without ever going back to review or question the foundations. Indeed when I was through America recently I even caught the suggestion that these questions are so uninteresting and unimportant that they can effectively be skipped altogether or introduced on the side. In fact when I originally proposed as a subject for a public lecture there another stone that I hereby give notice I would like to drop into the scholarly pond, called 'the priority of John', it was politely indicated to me that this would attract but a minuscule audience of New Testament specialists. Yet I happen to believe the Fourth Gospel is every bit as relevant for the Jesus of history as for the Christ of faith, as well as being of great interest to the layman, and if we have ignored or played down its evidence at this point it is important that we come to terms with the fact one way or the other. At any rate I would guard this concern for history and historicity as vital to the roots of Christology and the Christian faith, and one of the places at which we must be genuinely open today.

So much for the two sticking-points. Now for the two stretching-points.

iii. Honesty to the fact that the Christ is bigger than Jesus and God is bigger than Christ

Lay audiences I find are very open to the first two points, but strangely closed to this. Yet I believe it is equally true to the New Testament evidence. The very term 'Christ' is in the first instance, of course, not Christian but Jewish. It soon became the proper name for Jesus, but it remains a title like 'the Buddha'. The Christ figure, like the Logos, is much wider than Jesus. It stands for whatever reveals, mediates, embodies the invisible, timeless mystery of *theos* in the finite, temporal and human. The Christ is God with us, or God in us, the manifestation of the divine in the human, or, as Jung put it, the God-image in us, the archetype of the self, consubstantial with God and man. The Christ in this sense covers a concern as wide as humanity, though the actual word Christ may appear to exclude the Hindu or Moslem, just as the actual word God may appear to exclude the Buddhist.

The New Testament message is that the Christ has appeared in Jesus, that in him the universal light of the Logos has been focused as in the burning-glass of a single historical human being. But even as a proper name Christ includes more than Jesus or anything limited to thirty years of this man's historical existence. It embraces the cosmic Christ, the heavenly Christ, the Christ incognito in the least of these, the Christ that is to be. Indeed half the New Testament message of the Christ is of the Parousia, which in effect says 'You ain't seen nothing yet'. Moreover, this Logos, decisively disclosed in Jesus, is seen by the New Testament writers as the light and life of *every* man. In his light we are enabled to see the light of God everywhere. It is not that outside him there is no light.

The New Testament message is that Jesus is the Christ, that the Christ you have been looking for, or, as Jung might have put, the Christ of the collective unconscious, is to be recognized in this man. But I believe that today we are being forced to state more carefully what we mean by this 'is'. Let me give an analogy I have used before. According to traditional Roman Catholic teaching the Roman Catholic church was quite simply the Holy Catholic Church and *vice versa*. The rest of us were 'out', our orders 'null and void'. Vatican II rephrased it more carefully. The two are to be conjoined not by a simple 'est'. It is not that the Holy Catholic Church *consists of* the Roman Catholic Church but that it *subsists in* the Roman Catholic Church – the true church is in it but also beyond it. Similarly I believe we must say that the Christ subsists in Jesus, not that the Christ consists of Jesus. To believe that God is best defined in Christ is not to believe that God is confined to Christ. Or, to use a distinction familiar to theologians, Jesus is *totus Christus* – he is the Christ through and through: his whole being is an open window into God. But he is not *totum Christi*, all of Christ, the entire manifestation of the Christ-figure. Similarly Christ is *totus deus*. As Michael Ramsay has put it, 'God is Christlike and in him there is no unChristlikeness at all.' But he is not *totum dei*, all there is of God to be seen in the world. This leaves me free to say as a Christian that he is for me the focus, the definitive revelation of all the scattered light of God reflected and refracted in many other images, that, as Paul put it, he is *the* image of the invisible God, in whom all my experience is given coherence and integration as in no other. But it does not require or indeed allow me to say that he is exclusively this, that there are no other faces or foci of the Christ except that which I have seen in Jesus nor other faces of God except the human face of God in Christ. No other task I believe is more urgent for the church than to learn how to restate its conviction of the centrality of Christ both in relation to other faiths and in relation to insights of modern psychology without on the one hand being imperialistic and triumphalist (which, let us face it, we were when in the period of Christendom we had it to ourselves) or lapsing into a helpless syncretism, in which all religions and all insights are as good as each other or can be regarded ultimately as saying the same thing (which they are not). This is one of the points at which we must be both humble and honest and at which a true theology must give us the tools of discrimination. And we shall not find them without engaging in the risk of genuine inter-faith and what Raymond Panikkar in his latest title calls *Intra-religious Dialogue*. But I need not pursue this further because I have tried to spell it out in my *Truth is Two-Eyed*, in particular in the chapter on the uniqueness of Christ.

iv. Honesty to the story-line wherever it may lead

The church has traditionally worked with a two-storeyed theology – of two natures, divine and human, joined in the God-man as layers lying one on top of the other. This has had its problems, not the least in relation to the knowledge of the incarnate Christ. How could Jesus at the same time both know as God and not know as man? That was a question in answer to which Cyril of Alexandria indulged in some complicated theological mathematics. Again, could he have come down from the cross? The traditional answer, up to the end of the last century, even in such a liberal and indeed humanistic treatment as Seeley's *Ecce Homo*, was that he could have but chose not to. But it is now becoming recognized that the New Testament speaks not of a two-storeyed theology, of a sort of bat-man, uniting two natures like oil and water, one of which was bound to come to the top, but of a man, a genuine historical individual, of whom two stories can and must be told – one 'according to the flesh', of everything that concerned his humanity, the other 'according to the Spirit', of his ultimate, divine significance.

Now these two stories use recognizably different languages – the one of ordinary scientific and historical description, which can be related to and tested by other scientific and historical descriptions, the second of metaphor, symbol and myth, which are not intended to serve as alternative or additional historical accounts but as ways of interpreting the divine significance *of* the history. Up to about a hundred years ago it was not necessary to be particularly careful or rigorous in distinguishing these story-lines, whether in reference to Adam or to Christ. Since then it is essential – if we are not to invite people to accept (or more often dismiss) as history what was never meant to be taken as scientific explanation or historical description. How important this is can be judged by the fact that if the conservatives had won a hundred years ago and we had not distinguished, and been able to hold together, the story-lines both of Genesis and of Darwin it would have been impossible with integrity to be both a scientist and a Christian today. The discrimination is obvious in theory but delicate in practice – not least in the New Testament, where the history is so much more important than, say, that of the Exodus; and there is room for much discernment and also genuine disagreement about what is intended to be taken at what level. Honesty consists in truly being open to follow the particular story-line, wherever it may lead.

To illustrate this, let me start with a relatively simple example – the ascension story. Most intelligent Christians today see that this belongs essentially to the divine, symbolic, mythological story – what Jesus is 'according to the Spirit'. Whatever may be the historical substratum of the memory of a last resurrection appearance to which the writer of Acts, alone of the New Testament witnesses, has attached it (elsewhere, even in Luke's own gospel, and as late as the Epistle of Barnabas, it is seen as part of the significance of Easter Day), the meaning of the story lies in the theological affirmation that Jesus is not only alive but Lord. It is the assertion of his ascendency. And the language – of angels in white, of clouds, of going up and coming down – is the recognized symbolism of theophany, derived from the Old Testament, which no one in the first century would have much difficulty in recognizing as poetry rather than prose. We can with complete honesty be free to assert that it is nothing to do with movement in space nor much to do with a moment in time. But people will legitimately differ as to how they take the story, some more at one level some more at another. What is disingenuous is to try and have it both ways, as I am sure many in the church unthinkingly do. For instance, let me cite a comment I have used before from a book review by J. B. Phillips. He complained of the author: 'He appears reluctant to accept the story as a literal fact of history and I cannot think why.' And he went on to quote with approval a remark by C. S. Lewis, 'How else could a physical tangible body leave the surface of this planet?' I would like to ask him: 'Do you then really think that he went on through space, passing out of the gravitational pull, first of the earth then of the sun, and that now after two thousand years even at the speed of light he is hardly *en route* to the Milky Way?'. Of course he doesn't. No one does. And yet there are many intelligent Christians who would be shocked if you said that 'he ascended into heaven' was not a 'literal' statement. This only shows how lazy much of our thinking is. Indeed I suspect most of us, if we are honest, try to have it both ways, and suppose that Jesus did literally go up in front of the disciples' eyes, but that directly he got out of sight it somehow ceased to be a physical event at all and the trip was called off! In the space-age it is vitally important to make it clear to people that we *don't* think Jesus was the first cosmonaut. The story-lines have got to be more rigorously distinguished if the 'old, old story' is not to be heard as saying something very different.

A more difficult example, but still relatively simple, is the virgin birth. Many Christians of course do accept this at the level of the human story-line, and they are still entirely free to do so. As with Adam and Eve, they were until recently under no great pressure to discriminate. As long as one could accept with Aristotelian and medieval science that the entire material substance of a person's humanity was derived from the mother's blood and that the father's seed simply provided the impulse or trigger that set it all in motion, it was possible to believe that Jesus was, as orthoxody required, 'complete in regard to his humanity' and received it all from Mary without requiring the creation of any new matter. Indeed St Thomas Aquinas specifically denies that this was involved in the miracle of the virgin birth. We now know that genetics works differently. We have to postulate that half his genes were special creations or, to put it crudely, fakes, made to look as though he took after someone on the male side (presumably Joseph) – whereas really of course he did not at all. It is all rather like God creating the rocks with fossils in them, to make it look as though evolution were true. And that was a position, however hopeful it looked as a refuge to some nineteenth-century churchmen, in which we can now see it was impossible to rest. It confounds the story-lines.

But the difficulties, so far from blocking faith, should I believe help us to recognize more clearly that the two stories with which the New Testament opens, of the genealogies, traced through Joseph, and that of Jesus's virginal conception by the Spirit, are clearly incompatible if taken as truths on the same level, as were those of Darwin and Genesis. They belong to different story-lines and represent expansions respectively of the early Christian formula that 'according to the flesh' (that is in everything that affects the human story-line) he is son of David, the end-term of a long process of nature and history stretching back to and behind the beginnings of life on this planet, but that according to the Spirit (from the point of view of the divine purpose) he is son of God, the very expression and reflection of his being and nature, and may not from that viewpoint be understood or explained *simply* as the product of heredity and environment. In other words Matthew and Luke are saying of him exactly what John is saying of Christians, that as sons of God, as children of a 'heavenly' birth, they are not to be accounted for in terms of the will of the flesh nor of the will of man but only of God (John 1.13) – though of course as human beings they are born like everyone else. Paul and John put it differently, in terms not of his heavenly conception but of his heavenly mission, using the alternative myth of pre-existence – though I think it is important to stress that neither of them speaks of his pre-existence as a person or human being. As such he was no more pre-existent than you or I, being born like any genuine member of the species *homo sapiens* out of the family of man and the womb of Israel. It is, I believe, vital today not to confuse the story-lines if we are not to deny his solidarity in the evolutionary process with the whole human race he came to save. The story of the 'genesis' of Jesus Christ, to use Matthew's term (1.1, 18), is no more supplying us with information about gynaecology than the first Genesis story is about geology. On the 'how' of the process we must in each case be prepared to be completely open. I certainly should not presume to *deny* that there could have been a special creation at the physical level (any more than that God could have created the rocks with the fossils in them). All I am saying is that scripture is not a source-book of such information. It says simply that Mary was 'found to be with child' and that the whole thing was, despite appearances, 'of the Holy Spirit' (Matt. 1.18).

Lastly let me give one more example, the most delicate of all, that of the empty tomb.

I believe we have to be open to the fact, at whatever threat to our scientific and historical presuppositions, that both story-lines are here involved and that they are inextricably intertwined. As in the ascension story, there are elements (like the figures in glistening robes, the supernatural earthquake, the angelic messages) which are clearly there to interpret the divine significance of these events, saying to us that again despite appearances 'God is in this'. But there are also other elements, spices and stones and sweat-cloths, which have no such conventionally recognizable function. They are there to describe how things were believed to have been found. I have never been persuaded of the line of many New Testament scholars, following Bultmann, that the empty tomb story is simply a later construction of the church to give objectification to a purely spiritual belief in the cross not as defeat but as victory. I believe the descriptions reflect the indelible memory, of which the early Christians were at first able to make very little, that this is how things were found on the third day. How or why the tomb was empty is another matter. The first reaction was that it had been tampered with, and they never in fact commit themselves to any *other* explanation of the 'how', of the scientific or historical process. What they became convinced about is that somehow, whatever happened, it was of God and not of man (hence the angelic messengers, etc.). On what precisely happened to the old body the descriptions remain entirely unspecific (unlike those of the later apocryphal gospels), and we should be content to be equally open and undogmatic.

But I still believe that we have to be prepared to follow that story-line as honestly as we can, wherever it leads. And I have become disconcertingly aware of late that I may be compelled to take into account a piece of evidence that all my natural scientific and historical assumptions would predispose me to dismiss. I mean the Shroud of Turin. I cannot here go into this in any detail and must refer to the chapter I contributed on 'The Shroud and the New Testament' to *Face to Face with the Turin Shroud* edited by Peter

Jennings. It is still, as I write this, premature to say what will finally emerge from the latest round of tests, let alone from the carbon 14 dating test that has yet to be done – and which must be decisive at any rate for the *in*authenticity of the cloth. But if it *were* to show that it really does go back to the first century AD, then I think it would be difficult to believe that it is the burial cloth of any other man. Otherwise, quite apart from the detailed correspondences of the image with the gospel accounts, why should it have been thought so valuable as to be preserved through such vicissitudes for all these centuries and why in the first place should it have been detached from the body it wrapped rather than disintegrate with it like any other shroud?

But if it should turn out to be genuine, it would raise a hornet's nest of questions. My interest in it has been largely for the light it could throw on the gospel accounts, and not least that of the Fourth Gospel, which it seems to elucidate and bear out at many points. In any case, whatever the outcome, it has forced me to an investigation of Jewish burial customs that has helped me to understand the details of the narrative much more clearly. And if the gospels should be shown to be trustworthy at this level here, then it must incline us to take them seriously for their historicity at other points. It would surely have to make scholars give up the supposition which on literary grounds I have never found credible, that the empty tomb itself was simply the creation of the church. But equally, if the Shroud were genuine, it certainly would not in my judgment add up to any kind of proof of resurrection, nor would it say anything decisive about the mode of it – even if the most likely hypothesis for explaining the image-formation did turn out to be some very brief moment of intense radiation from the body itself. That must await further investigation. Nothing in my faith hangs on it, and it would place nothing beyond doubt or faith. On the other hand, if authenticated, it ought to make a difference to unbelief, to the dismissiveness of many both within and outside the church. Meanwhile, until the trail goes dead, it has awakened in me a curiosity which honesty tells me that I must be prepared to follow till proved otherwise. Certainly it is a new and fascinating point of contact between the two story-lines, but one at which much discrimination is necessary if once again we are not to confuse them in the deductions we draw.

IV

WHAT IS THE GOSPEL?

This is a question to which one might think there should be a single clear answer. After all, if Christians cannot speak with one voice at this point, why should they expect anyone to listen? Yet not only do they not so speak, but I shall argue that they should not. Or, if they did, it would be a sure sign that they'd got it too small.

Ask, What is the gospel? and you will get a bewildering variety of answers. In general no doubt the answers will be complementary, but at certain points of emphasis also contradictory. For a plurality is essential if we are to be true to the fullness of the truth as it is in Jesus. The gospel condemns and judges *any* of our particular understandings of it. To state it in cut-and-dried terms is bound to be reductionist – the very charge usually brought against those who refuse to state it in cut-and-dried terms.

Let us begin by sitting under St Paul's statement of it in Eph. 3.7–10, an epistle which even if he did not pen it (and I am more than ever persuaded he did) remains what has been called 'the crown of Paulinism'.

> Such is the gospel of which I was made a minister, by God's gift, bestowed unmerited on me in the working of his power. To me, who am less than the least of all God's people, he has granted of his grace the privilege of proclaiming to the Gentiles the good news of the unfathomable riches of Christ, and of bringing to light how this hidden purpose was to be put into effect. It was hidden for long ages in God the creator of the universe, in order that now, through the church, the wisdom of God in all its varied

forms might be made known to the rulers and authorities in the realms of heaven.

From that we may note three phrases: (1) The gospel is the good news of the 'unfathomable' riches of Christ – *anexichniaston*, literally, 'not to be tracked out'. It is the word used in the book of Job for the unsearchable ways of God. What Christ means cannot be plotted, caught in a grid or mapped. (2) The mystery is 'hidden', wrapped from long ages in the purposes of God. One could adapt the words of Lao Tzu of the *tao*: 'The gospel that can be spoken (or put into words) is not the eternal gospel.' (3) It is the wisdom of God 'in all its varied forms', *polypoikilos*, 'many-faceted', like a diamond shining in different lights.

J. B. Phillips once wrote a book saying to Christians *Your God is Too Small*. So this passage says to each and every one of us: Your gospel is too small – however you state it. And nowhere in fact over the whole range of Christian vocabulary have our words become what Eliot called so 'thoroughly small and dry'. The very term 'the gospel' so far from being common coin in the secular world, expressing the outreach of Christian truth, is confined largely to Christian in-talk. Again, if we plan these days to have a 'mission' in Cambridge the first, and in my experience also the last, thing we have to do is to cast around for another word for it – so that the very name will not put people off before it starts. And 'missions', in the plural, as in the phrase 'giving to missions', is equally unusable. Finally there is little doubt, in my mind at least, that our image of 'evangelism' must go. This is not because I am against evangelism, but precisely because I am for it. Yet the sort of literature that used to bombard the clergy from the Archbishops' Council on Evangelism – it seems to have stopped of late – had the effect of making me curl up rather than open out. This was a reflex mechanism: I couldn't help it. It reminded me of an experiment I tried once on the spur of the moment round a roomful of people in San Francisco, a mixed-up cross-section of humanists and Christians, Protestants and Catholics. Two phrases came up in the discussion, each of them seeking to communicate the basic Christian experience of justification by faith. One was Tillich's 'Accept the fact that you are accepted', the other 'Accept Jesus Christ as your personal Lord and Saviour'. On the face of it, the latter is the more 'evangelistic', presenting what many would regard as the heart of the gospel more explicitly. Yet, without exception, everyone round that room found that the former turned them on while the latter turned them off, actually making them sheer away from the truth it embodied. It was much the same for many with the Archbishops' 'Call to the Nation' a few years back, on which an observer of my acquaintance commented, 'I did not think before that it was possible to be both vacuous and divisive at the same time'! I am sure it was entirely well meant. But if such is the unintended effect it does seem important to ask, What has gone wrong?

I believe it is that almost all our images, our stereotypes, of the gospel and of evangelism are limited and therefore limiting. Consider a few, from the different bands of the ecclesiastical spectrum.

Let us start from those who would call themselves evangelicals. For they have made evangelism their 'thing'. Indeed most people would find it difficult to distinguish between the meaning of the words 'evangelistic' and 'evangelical'. If you talk about evangelism it is *their* image of it that is immediately conveyed – Billy Graham and all that. I happen to know and admire Billy Graham personally and I have seen quite a bit of him recently, and I know that he is a good deal bigger than his image, in directions that many evangelicals would find surprising and perhaps disturbing. But it is the stereotype that I am concerned with. And in such circles 'preaching the gospel' tends to signify something quite clear and distinct. It is conceived fairly narrowly, individualistically, often anti-intellectually and anti-critically, and if the message is not formulated in a certain recognizable idiom it is suspected as unsound.

Above all, 'preaching the gospel' is contrasted with getting involved in 'the social gospel'. Politicization is the great diversion and corruption. Of course it is always tacitly understood that politics means left-wing politics. Preserving the *status quo* is apolitical, and even Thatcherite monetarism, making an 'ism' of the money supply, can be packaged and commended as the pure prayer of St Francis! But at a less rarified level let me illustrate this attitude from a trivial incident in Cambridge. Recently our Third World lunch in Trinity, organized by the College Union, was in aid of a Christian collective farm in Sri Lanka, and to my agreeable surprise the Christian Union said that they would also put the profits from their weekly lunch towards it. By good fortune we were able to have with us towards the end of term the Sinhalese Anglican priest who founded it. And he described vividly the struggle into which they had inexorably been drawn, alongside Buddhists and Marxists, if the poor were to feed themselves at all, for basic peasant land-rights – largely against British-dominated tea-planting interests. When later I asked the treasurer of the College Union whether the money had been sent he said he had been waiting for the Christian Union contribution; but now they had gone back on it 'because it was too political'. I am afraid I went away muttering tight-lipped, 'Typical', and registering one more defeat for the gospel. They doubtless warm as much as their fellow-evangelicals to singing Timothy Dudley-Smith's stirring setting of the Magnificat based on the New English Bible:

> . . . powers and dominions lay their glory by;
> Proud hearts and stubborn wills are put to flight,
> The hungry fed, the humble lifted high.

But here was action, or rather inaction, whose effect was precisely to leave the powerful and intractable securely in possession – and anything that does that is not the gospel.

In most cases I am sure this failure to present what I, but not they, would mean by 'the full gospel' is quite innocent. Indeed I have been forced, as I said earlier, to conclude that most evangelicals including liberal ones (a man like my successor at Woolwich, David Sheppard, now Bishop of Liverpool, is a notable exception) are political innocents; and this is because their gospel fails to include a real theology of the *world*, of matter and power, and therefore of politics. This was brought home by the first number I stumbled on of the magazine *Sojourners*, which represents the great counterblast to all this from inside the evangelical camp. It gave a discerning, and devastating, analysis from within the Southern Baptist evangelical tradition of why Jimmy Carter was politically so ineffectual – precisely because of the limitations of the understanding of the gospel in which he had been nurtured: it simply had no theology of power.

But before leaving this image of evangelism let me mention one other phenomenon of it, particularly in some of its extremer transatlantic versions, which seems to me far from innocent and indeed very vicious. One of the conversations I most vividly remember in Israel was with a highly cultured and spiritually sensitive Quaker, who was an Arab Christian. 'Shall I tell you', she said, 'who our real enemies are? They are not the Muslims among whom we live and with whom we get on well enough. They are not even the Jews who constantly harry us and make our life impossible [and incidentally drive even pacifists like herself back upon the PLO]. No, they are Christians from the West [and she meant American evangelical fundamentalists] who so define the fulfilment of the biblical "prophecies" as to leave us Arab Christians no place for existence.'

They play straight into the hands of Zionist propaganda, which, as I saw later in the States, exploits it gratefully in whole-page advertisements in the American press. If they don't know what they are doing, they are not easily to be forgiven: for the price of their theological naivety is paid in other peoples' lives.

But most of this image of the gospel is not gospel not because it is vicious but because it is vacuous – as I said earlier, it curls one up. Here is an example from the latest tract to reach me, unsolicited, from the self-styled World Evangelism International Headquarters. 'If you are interested', they say, 'in spreading the Gospel to the unsaved', you can obtain 'small anointed messages written under the inspiration of God by our beloved Brother' and cassettes of 'outstanding inspirational messages', the latest of which is entitled *Fellowshipping God*. Ugh!

I dredge this up not to caricature this image but to explain why any understanding of the gospel that can produce such fruits is for many a positive dissuasive. If this, or anything remotely like it, is evangelism, then it is not surprising that lots of people run a mile to avoid being button-holed.

But, secondly, let me turn briefly to the opposite pole, that of the catholic counterpart. Catholics, whether Anglican or Roman, don't *talk* so much about evangelism, but of course they would be the first to say that they have the same, one gospel to present. And it is a version of it which, biblically speaking, has one great advantage over the other, namely, that the church is seen not just as a corollary of the gospel ('Accept Jesus Christ as your personal Lord and Saviour' – and then join up with others who do) but as an integral part of its content. The gospel *is* the new life 'in Christ Jesus', and that for the New Testament is inescapably corporate. As Oliver Quick put it in one of his titles many years ago, it is *The Gospel of the New World*. And therein lies also the seed by which the limitations of this presentation must be judged. For something begins to go wrong when the gospel of the new world, of the kingdom, *becomes* the gospel of the church, so that the church – its life, its sacraments, its ministrations – is seen not merely as the medium but as the message; and the centre of the new life is for practical purposes equated with the circumference. For at this point the church is no longer judged by the kingdom, and ecclesiastical absolutism becomes the shadow-image of biblical fundamentalism. And when these two extremes meet nothing is calculated to reduce my faith and my hope and my charity so quickly.

Finally, in these stereotypes or reduced images of the gospel we must not omit that of the liberals. Indeed it is they more than others who these days are charged with reductionism. And I confess that at the heart of much they say there is for me not much gospel either. I have recently been sitting at Cambridge through a fascinating course of Hulsean Lectures on the English Modernists – the story of the Modern Churchman's Union, Bishop Barnes, and all that. My sympathies have been with their intellectual courage, but on the whole (there were great exceptions like Charles Raven) they do not seem to have had much fire in their belly. They were accused by their opponents of presenting 'the gospel of negativity', and a more bloodless expression of it 'sicklied o'er with the pale cast of thought' one could often hardly imagine. It was said of them, unfairly, that the question from which they started was 'What will Jones swallow?' When similarly charged myself, I used to reply with William Temple, 'No. I am Jones asking what there is to eat.' And a genuine concern for what of the old fare was edible, for what in it really was good news, did underlie the work of the liberals and of the radicals after them. This was true of a book like Paul Van Buren's *The Secular Meaning of the Gospel* or Thomas Altizer's *Gospel of Christian Atheism.* Such men were acutely aware from contact with their contemporaries that much if not most of 'God'-language had for them 'gone dead'. And their laudable concern was E. M. Forster's 'Only connect'. Equally Bultmann's demythologizing of the New Testament started with his attempts to preach the gospel to German soldiers during the war. It was the same, I believe, more recently with the authors of *The Myth of God Incarnate.* They were conscious that the gospel was becoming for many, themselves included, incredible. Nevertheless I cannot really believe that 'the gospel of Christian atheism', or 'Christianity without Incarnation?', or the giving up of any claim for the uniqueness of Christ, or the uncritical identification of Christianity with secular humanism or political liberation (thus giving Eric Mascall or Edward Norman their toe-holds) are anything but impoverishments of the gospel. They are in danger of leaving nothing at the centre distinctive or strong enough to live by, let alone to die for.

While the first two stereotypes of the gospel have in their own way strong centres but hard edges, this version has characteristically a soft centre with open edges. My increasing conviction, as I said earlier, is that one must have a strong centre – both biblical and catholic – with the edges and the ends gloriously and liberatingly open.

Having sketched some of the stereotypes that limit the gospel and simply stop it *being* gospel for many, let me now try to say positively what I believe it is. One cannot do better than begin with the phrase with which it is introduced in St Mark (1.14f.), the gospel of the kingdom of God, of the letting loose of God's sovereign righteousness and love into the affairs of men. And St Luke spells this out by the sermon of Jesus which he sets as it were as the frontispiece of his gospel (4.16–30): the manifesto of good news to the poor, of release to the prisoners, of recovery of sight to the blind and of letting the broken go free. This of course is a deliberate citation of the Old Testament, in which Jesus takes up and makes his own its vision of 'salvation', wholeness, *shalom*, which is far larger than that to which the biblicists have reduced it by their question 'Are you saved?'. It is a making whole which includes body, mind and spirit, the individual and the corporate, the personal and the political. In fact how anyone who reads the Bible could have supposed there could be a gospel which was *not* a 'social gospel' defeats me. The very need for the latter term, used these days derogatively, shows how far we have departed from scriptural holiness. The gospel of the wisdom of God is indeed many-faceted and, as Jesus once said in irony to those who would play off one face against another, 'justified of all her children' (Luke 7.35), or, as the Good News Bible puts it, 'shown to be true by all who accept it' – and an incredibly varied lot they are. Only that can be the gospel which is as large as the Christ in whom all things cohere (Col. 1.17). Or, as St Paul also put it, 'To me *life* is Christ' (Phil. 1.21): 'all human life is there' – transformed.

There are no bounds or edges to the gospel; but what is the centre? Again one could sum it up by using a formula of St Paul's: 'the grace of our Lord Jesus Christ and the love of God and the fellowship of the Holy Spirit'. Nothing could be more biblical or more catholic than that – even though 'the Trinity' might seem the remotest thing from a 'gospel message' to the vicar struggling with his sermon for Trinity Sunday! This incidentally illustrates how almost every 'doctrine', whether of the Trinity or the Atonement or the Fall or the Ministry, is today a liability to the reality it seeks to communicate. The containers have to be cracked if the quick centre, in all its simplicity and profundity, is to be released. The last thing I want to do is to depreciate doctrine. It has got to be reworked continuously – and I myself have tried to do my share, for instance, on Christology and the Last Things. But I find myself constantly wanting to say that I believe, and believe passionately, in incarnation, in atonement, in ministry and the rest *before* going on to give them a capital letter and put a definite article in front of them. What I believe about 'the Trinity' I confess that I know less and less – and most of the available models are in trouble. But I want at all costs to hold to and communicate 'the grace of our Lord Jesus Christ and the love of God and the fellowship of the Holy Spirit' as the heart and concentrate of the gospel.

So let me, very briefly, end by unpacking something of that formula.

1. 'The grace of our Lord Jesus Christ'. The impression left by the sermon of Jesus at Nazareth was summed up as 'the words of grace that fell from his lips' – at whatever level people understood that; and some no doubt went out saying 'That was a lovely sermon'! Again St Paul says to his readers, 'You know the grace, or the graciousness, of our Lord Jesus Christ: he was rich, yet for your sake he became poor, so that through his poverty you might become rich' (II Cor. 8.9). And he sums up his gospel by saying, 'It is by grace you are saved, through faith in him; it is not your own doing' (Eph. 2.8). This on any showing is the heart of the Christian message, what St Paul calls justification by faith, but which is spelt out so much more vividly by Jesus in the incomparable stories of the Pharisee and the publican or the prodigal son or in his dealings with the Samaritan woman or the woman taken in adultery. The gospel is sheer grace – yet never cheap grace – liberating men and women to *live* – at every level of their being, in every context, individual or social. It is what the Jesus of St John calls eternal life, abundant life, real life.

2. 'The love of God'. 'God so loved the world that he gave' (John 3.16): this is the great evangelical text. And everything we have to preach is grounded in this love, the love that loves us before we love him (I John 4.19), that dies for us while we are yet sinners (Rom. 5.8), and from which nothing in all creation can separate (Rom. 8.38f.). And it is of this all-embracing divine reality that St Paul writes in the same chapter of Ephesians from which we started, that 'with deep roots and firm foundations, may you be strong to grasp, with all God's people, what is the breadth and length and height and depth of the love of Christ, and to know it, though it is beyond knowledge' (3.17–19). 'Pure universal love thou art', said Charles Wesley. Or, in the words of another great hymn-writer, F. W. Faber, 'The love of God is broader than the measures of man's mind.' But, he went on, 'We make his love too narrow by false limits of our own'. Indeed the very belief in universalism, that God's love is ultimately more powerful to draw than man's will, any

man's, to resist, is itself regarded by many within the church as severing the nerve of evangelism – there must be a cut-off somewhere, either at the moment of death or by insisting that some, perhaps most, will be damned for ever. Yet the vision of the consummation, that God will be all in all as love (I Cor. 15.28), that there is nothing in heaven or earth or under the earth that shall not confess Jesus as Lord (Phil. 2.10f.), that Christ fills the universe and must come into everything (Eph. 4.10), that as no aspect of life lies outside his rule so none lies outside the Christian's concern, that though God, again, may be defined in Jesus he cannot be confined to him (or to Christianity) – all these are convictions which I believe to be corollaries of a genuinely full gospel.

3. Finally, 'the fellowship of the Holy Spirit'. This is the infectious centre of the new life – what Paul Van Buren spoke of so splendidly as the 'contagious freedom' of Easter. This is the gospel of 'the new world' – of the reality tasted by those in whom, as F. W. Robertson put it a century ago, 'the resurrection begun makes the resurrection credible'. This is why what William Temple called 'the great new fact' of the universal church is itself an integral part of the good news, its quick centre and its point of sale. Or rather it should be. For again one can see how the *koinonia* or common ownership in Holy Spirit, participation in the powers of the age to come, gets narrowed down to describe *a* community, 'the fellowship' of the religious club, or sentimentalized into 'having fellowship' (let alone 'fellowshipping God') until it ends by being measured out in cups of tea and sugar-spoons. The message becomes the medium – whereas there is a true sense in which the medium is the message. The church, as that great New Testament scholar Sir Edwyn Hoskyns once said, is 'the concretization of the grace of our Lord Jesus Christ and the love of God and the fellowship of the Holy Spirit'. This is where it should all be made visible and made local – though perhaps his metaphor was an unfortunate one. For it suggests, as alas is so often the case, that this is where it is set in concrete, in God's frozen people!

Yet never let us forget that the church is only the medium, the medium of the kingdom. It is 'through the church', as St Paul said in that great passage from Ephesians, that 'the wisdom of God in all its varied forms' has to be made known to the powers that rule this world (Eph. 3.10). And throughout the Bible the people of God is constantly judged by the reign of God of which it is the instrument. The instrument has been discarded once and can be discarded again; and God can and does work outside it. To evangelize is to seek to elicit the confession, in word and action, singly and structurally, that 'Jesus is Lord'. Yet the kingdom is not composed of those who say 'Lord, Lord'. There are many who shall come from east and west, from other religions or none, who have never 'known' him or named the name. And these will judge our petty proselytizing understandings of evangelism whether at home or abroad. So it is that some of the most sensitive theologians of the church in our day, both Catholic and Protestant, have found themselves driven to speak, however inadequately, of 'anonymous Christians' and 'the latent church'. One of the great Christian novels of our age (yes, I would call it that though it mentions the name of Jesus but once) is Petru Dumitriu's *Incognito*, and he has recently written a moving spiritual autobiography, yet to be translated, under the title *Au Dieu Inconnu*. This does not mean that we do not have to say with St Paul that 'what you worship but do not know, this is what I proclaim' (Acts 17.23). Yet we can do it in such a way that the name-tag becomes a price-tag with precisely the opposite effect. Sydney Carter, if I may cite him again, may be heard protesting for many in our day with his poem 'Anonymous':

> The Jesus who
>
> keeps saying 'I am Jesus,
> look at me,
> there is no substitute'
>
> is an impostor. Do not trust
> the Christian cult of
> personality, I came
>
> to turn you on and not
> to turn you off,
> to make you free and not
>
> to tie you up.
> My yoke was easy and
> my burden light
>
> until they made
> salvation copyright, and
> all in the name of Jesus.

And I ended my *Human Face of God* in which I quoted that with the comment, 'Only if the copyright registered once, on behalf of all, in Jesus is not reserved can Christ be the man for all, the human face of God'.

I have sought to speak as best I know – and, as Wittgenstein said, whereof we know not we must be silent – about what the angel in the book of Revelation flying in mid-heaven called the 'eternal gospel' (Rev. 14.6). But unfortunately – or fortunately – we do not fly in mid-heaven. We are earthed, living in a particular time and culture, and the Christ who is 'the same yesterday, today, and for ever' (Heb. 13.8) can be that only by becoming, as Kierkegaard said, the contemporary of every generation, by being *our* Christ. We have constantly to ask with Bonhoeffer: 'Who is Christ for us today?' It is impossible to answer in the abstract the question, What is the gospel? – as though there were some timeless 'essence of Christianity'. An essence of beef, or of anything else, is the same as an extract, an abstraction. Indeed whenever I am asked a question about essence I want, with Kierkegaard, to ask one back about existence, just as Jesus, when asked 'Who is my neighbour?', told a story which never answered it but posed the much more searching question, Who was neighbour, who proved neighbour, to the man who fell into the hands of the robbers? (Luke 10.29–37). So instead of knocking the question endlessly around, What is the gospel?, I would close by asking, What *is* gospel – for you? What for you, in the words of the negro spiritual, is 'joy, joy, joy'? What really makes you tick, both 'in the flesh and in the Lord' (Philem. 16), or as the NEB renders it, 'as a man and as a Christian'? Or, rather, we must learn to say, as a human being and as a Christian. For if you are a woman – or your skin is black or your belly is empty – you may answer that question disconcertingly differently. Even the gospel is contextual. 'Liberation theology', it has been said, 'is the form which liberal theology has taken in the third world', with the corollary that 'liberation theology cannot be imported directly into the first world without distortion' (Paul Gibson, 'A Partisan Appeal for a Liberal Mission' in *Theology*, May 1979). The questions change the answers. Let us never forget too that within the presentation of the one gospel there is room, in all pain and mutual forbearance, for Blake's comment:

> The vision of Christ that thou dost see
> Is my vision's greatest enemy.

This is all part of what it takes to live with and be judged by 'the good news of the unfathomable riches of Christ' and 'the wisdom of God in all its varied forms'. May we never knowingly undersell it, even for the sake of gaining converts, by reducing it to our own image.

V

SOCIAL ETHICS AND THE WITNESS OF THE CHURCH

What follows was first given as a contribution to a conference on 'Christian Ecumenical Witness on Moral Issues' organized by the Franciscan Friars of the Atonement at Westminster Cathedral in October 1976. The issue of how the church can speak with a united voice, especially on ethics and especially with Roman Catholics, has since been rendered still more problematic by the utterances of Pope John Paul II. His 'hard line' on clerical celibacy, the laicization of priests desiring to get married, the ordination of women, contraception, abortion and nullity (all at which at bottom have something to do with sex) has reinforced the appeal 'consent' rather 'consensus'. However much Anglicans may admire him on other issues, we must, I believe, resist this appeal in the name and for the sake of a wider catholicity. It reflects, I suspect, in large degree the cultural gap between Eastern Europe and the liberal West, and most Roman Catholics I meet are equally dismayed by it. The disaster would be if ecumenical dialogue were to be stifled at this point. But fortunately there is little sign of this happening.

Let me start with three quotations from three different ecclesiastical traditions, to store away and think about. I offer them not for their immediate application to the present discussion, though they are, I am sure, relevant at a deeper level, but because over the years they have stuck in my mind and I find myself going back to the distinctions they raise in an area where above all what St Paul calls discernment or discrimination (*to diaphorein*) is perhaps the greatest gift and most searching test of the Spirit.

The first is from the Russian Orthodox theologian, Nicolas Berdyaev, whose work is overdue for revaluation: 'Bread for myself is a material problem: bread for other people is a spiritual problem.' That may help to sort out those who question whether social ethics is a part, or at any rate a priority, of the gospel at all.

The second is from the French Protestant André Philippe, at that time a member of de Gaulle's Free French government in exile: 'I am a Christian socialist. I am not a socialist because I am a Christian. I am anti-capitalist because I am a Christian. I am a socialist because I am a professor of economics.' That may help to sort out – though it is too simplistic to solve – the questions in this field arising from the relation between moral and technical judgments.

The third is from the Anglican William Temple, writing as Archbishop of York in his *Christianity and Social Order*, recently republished with an introduction by a former Prime Minister, Mr Edward Heath:

> At the end of this book I shall offer, in my capacity as a Christian citizen, certain proposals for definite action which would, in my private judgment, conduce to a more Christian ordering of society; but if any member of the Convocation of York should be so ill-advised as to table a resolution that these proposals be adopted as a political programme for the Church, I should in my capacity as Archbishop resist that proposal with all my force, and should probably, as President of the Convocation, rule it out of order.

That may help to sort out the questions of what in this area the church should pronounce upon as the church in contrast with what its members should say as individual citizens – and the related and equally delicate questions of what a clergyman or bishop has the right or the duty to say *from the pulpit.*

I have chosen to begin this way because Christian ecumenical witness on moral issues is confused and confounded more often I believe by divergences of approach than by differences of content. Of course there are areas where Catholics and Protestants have stood and still stand for very different things, most obviously on matters of sex, which, though crucial to persons and their wholeness, have been allowed to loom too large, in my judgment, not only in the eyes of the world but in the time-tables of the church. It is a case of 'these things ought ye to have done, and not left the others undone' (Matt. 23.23). Yet I suspect that in practice ecumenical co-operation has been weakened not so much by irreconcilable differences of goal but, psychologically, by divergent points of departure and disparate casts of mind.

The traditional Roman Catholic approach to this as to other issues has been 'from above'. The church's social teaching has percolated down, through encyclicals and other pronouncements, and the problem has been that of *consent*. 'So often', if I may cite the dilemma as it was posed to me by the organizer of this conference, 'one wonders whether the individual really believes in the Church's teaching, or [accepts it] because of an "official" document produced from above and imposed on the faithful.'

The traditional Protestant approach, and on these issues this includes the Anglican, is much more 'from below', and the problem is that of *consensus*. Perhaps I may illustrate this not from the contemporary moral debate but from Bishop J. B. Lightfoot addressing the issues of his day at the Durham Diocesan Conference just two months before his death in 1889. He said this:

> Of all the manifold blessings which God has showered on our English Church, none is surely greater than the providence which has shielded her from premature and authoritative statements, which soon or late must be repudiated or explained away, however great may have been the temptation from time to time. The Church of England is nowhere directly or indirectly committed to the position that the sun goes round the earth; or that this world has only existed for six or seven thousand years; or that the days of creation are days of twenty-four hours each; or that the scriptual genealogies must always be accepted as strict and continuous records of the descent from father to son; or that the sacred books were written in every case by those whose names they bear; or that there is nowhere allegory, which men have commonly mistaken for history. On these and similar points our Church has been silent; though individuals, even men of high authority, have written hastily or incautiously.

He did not instance moral questions, nor did he say whether he would include popes among 'individuals of high authority', but I think the point is made. We have been saved from much! Nor did he give examples of where church bodies *have* pronounced on issues where time may suggest a more discriminating stance. But at least in the Church of England we can say that we were wrong (or let us say right for that time) and can change our less than infallible rulings.

But rather than concentrate on issues where the church has, rightly or wrongly, pronounced from above – like Anglicans on divorce or Methodists on drink – let me explore the problems arising for a united moral witness of the approach from below. These, as I said, are not so much those of consent as of consensus. The weakness, as well of course as the strength, of this approach is the plethora and apparent confusion of voices. Mr Enoch Powell claims to speak as a convinced high Anglican, but no one, least of all himself, identifies his line with that of the Church of England. The same was true of the 'Red Dean' of Canterbury, though abroad the distinction between Dean and Archbishop was not understood, to Dr Fisher's chagrin and often, one suspects, to Dr Johnson's delight. But, to come nearer home, recent issues of *Crucible*, the journal of the Church of England's Board of Social Responsibility, were enlivened, if not electrified, by a devastating analysis of a report on the state of the nation commissioned by the editor – who is also secretary of the Board that commissioned the report! This officially instigated debate between two leading Anglicans seems to me thoroughly healthy and I am grateful to belong to a church in which it can take place. But it may make others despair.

Yet let us probe a little deeper. What is it that makes fellow-Christians differ so disconcertingly on moral, social and political issues, so that the world must often wonder whether being Christian makes any difference to our pronouncements at all? I am not alone in discovering a good deal more common ground on social issues with many of my libertarian, humanist and even Marxist friends than with many fellow-churchmen. How can these things be? Is it simply an abdication of any common Christian witness, a declaration to the world of our moral bankruptcy? Does it reduce what we can say together to the level of untheological platitude or moralizing exhortation? I do not think so. It means I believe that we must learn to discern and to discriminate between the levels at which we are speaking – or more often feeling. For the points of greatest confusion – and contusion – are usually those 'gut' issues of life and death, race and sex, where our reaction is instinctively evoked more by our being-in-the-flesh than by our being-in-Christ.

Since I have introduced this Pauline distinction, let me pursue it. St Paul recognizes that as Christians we still live in the flesh (*en sarki*). The position from which we judge moral, social and political issues will inevitably and properly be that in which we are placed by nature and shaped by all the forces and pressures of heredity and environment. This is simply a God-given formation, and is morally neutral. It was true even of Jesus himself, and it is part of what we mean by his being fully human, though this has often been denied or slurred over. He was a Jew of the first century with all the built-in attitudes, prejudices and frustrations which being a Jew of the first century included – towards women, towards Samaritans and Gentiles, towards the occupying power and its quisling agents. The wonder of him was not that he did not start with these sentiments but that he overcame them – and that not without an internal struggle, as the incident of the Canaanite woman (Matt.15.21–8) and the Epistle to the Hebrews bring out.

We all look out on our world from the place and time where nature has set us. I am a white, English, twentieth-century, middle-aged, middle-class, heterosexual male – and there is nothing I can do about it. It will condition, and has conditioned, all my attitudes. And over the years certain syndromes develop so that on issues, say, of power and powerlessness, quality versus equality, freedom versus order, one comes instinctively to give precedence to certain values over other values. These are the things that make us little liberals or little conservatives. We have different perspectives and with these perspectives some things loom larger than others, whether as goals or blockages, and determine our moral, social and political priorities. That is why Christians can, and thankfully do, look at things so differently, and why democracy is so vital to a sinful and civilized society. So far from it being a weakness that there are Christians in every party and every social movement, it is a strength; and, to adapt Lightfoot again, 'of all the manifold blessings which God has showered on our English nation' few are surely greater than the absence of Christian political parties.

Our being – and therefore our being divided – 'in the flesh' is a fact of life which we should neither deprecate nor wish to depreciate. To try as Christians to deny it or cover it up as evil or unreal is to show ourselves Gnostics. But, says St Paul, there is all the difference in the world between our being-in-the-flesh and allowing this fact to determine our whole attitude. It is the contrast between 'walking in the flesh' (*en sarki*) and 'warring according to the flesh' (*kata sarka*). And let me illustrate that contrast from one of those 'gut' areas of life where St Paul does not analyse himself but where we can and, if we are not to be fundamentalists, must. I refer to his attitude to women, on which he regularly gets what today would be called a 'bad press'.

St Paul was not only a typical Jewish rabbi of his time but one who on his own admission gave preference to the celibate life. He accepted the subordination and, though there is more doubt on this, enjoined the silence of women even within the church. Indeed we may go on to say, though I do not think this is really evidenced, that he had all sorts of hang-ups on the subject of women. But let us pile on the prejudices from which he started. It makes it only the more astonishing that he came through, not only to a view of sexual relations which is infinitely more balanced and sensitive than the wrenching of the phrase 'It is better to marry than to burn' (I Cor. 7.9) has suggested, but to a conviction that in Christ, not indeed the difference, but discrimination between male and female is utterly and absolutely out. In this he was far more radical than the church has shown itself even to this day. And the reason why the church has taken so long to draw the implications of his insights on this or on slavery has again been the conditioning imposed by its position in society, 'in the flesh'. There is nothing as such wrong in this. Time and place, culture and climate, determine what is socially, politically and indeed theologically possible. Here is one last quotation which I have used before, this time from the German Catholic monk Klaus Klostermaier:

> Theology at 120° in the shade seems very different from theology at 70°. The theologian at 70° in a good position presumes God to be happy and contented, well-fed and rested, without needs of any kind. The theologian at 120° tries to imagine a God who is hungry and thirsty, who suffers and is sad, who sheds perspiration and knows despair.

Yet temperature, which can make theology in one respect more radical, can make it in another more conservative. It is noticeable for instance that the pressure for the ordination of women comes much more from the first world than the third, from WASPS (White Anglo-Saxon Protestants) than from blacks – and from the second world (frozen ecclesiastically as well as physically) hardly at all!

But once we allow this natural conditioning to become spiritually conforming we fall into what St Paul calls 'the mind of the flesh' (*to phronēma tēs sarkos*): we let our outlook be determined, not only begun but bounded, by our being in the world. And that is 'enmity to God' (Rom. 8.7); and it must be withstood if necessary, as Paul himself withstood Peter, 'to the face' (Gal. 2.11). Thus, to pursue the example I gave, I would say that *for us*, given our insights into the blasphemy of 'the great white male upon the throne', sexism is now as much of a contradiction of the gospel as racism. And I am bound to go on to say that for me denial of Holy Orders on grounds of sex alone *is* sexism and cannot be redeemed from being such by any appeal to tradition. I will not speak for others and I may not condemn my fellow-Christians who judge differently, if, as St Paul says on another issue, their judgment is grounded in conscience and not prejudice. Yet let us remember that, with all his forbearance towards the weaker brother, he ends that debate with the words that 'anything which does not arise from conviction (*pistis*) is sin' (Rom. 14.23) – though he closes another equally delicate discussion with the humility and openness to correction which we should never forget in Christ: 'I *think* that I also have the Spirit of God' (I Cor. 7.40).

Moreover he starts the famous passage which grounds this humility in the example of Jesus (Phil. 2.5–11) with words on which I would end, because, properly translated, as I believe, they sum up what I want to say. In the familiar version they run: 'Have this mind in you which was also in Christ Jesus.' But the verb 'was', and therefore the past tense, is not in the Greek, and I think the NEB is right in taking them in a different sense: 'Let your bearing towards one another arise out of your life in Christ Jesus.' In other words, let your being-in-Christ rather than your being-in-the-world, with *its* priorities and values, mould your entire mind or outlook. When, and always alas to the degree that, *that* happens, we shall come, as he says, not to the 'same mind' (as the NEB here I believe wrongly translates) but to 'one mind' (Phil. 2.2). It is a unity in and of the Spirit which can allow for and take up – while at the same time softening and transforming – the natural and God-given differences of the flesh without being broken by them. He concludes: 'Let us then keep to this way of thinking, those of us who are mature. If there is any point on which you think differently, this also God will make plain to you. Only let your conduct be consistent with the level we have already reached' (Phil. 2.15f.). And that 'only' clause is important, socially as well as individually. Reversion, even to first-century social stereotypes, whether of sex or slavery or anything else, is sin.

Christian maturity is a pluriform and a growing thing. Especially in a time of rapid social change it is, I believe, incompatible with a static or hierarchical concept of authority. We live in a time of what Van Buren has called 'the dissolution of the absolute' in the old monolithic sense – and no Curia playing Canute can will it back. Yet the complementarity of the personal and corporate, in contrast with the antinomy between the individual and collective, provides, I am convinced, the raw material of a richer *consensus fidelium.* It will not be achieved without many tensions and necessary conflicts, nor without creative leadership theological and ecclesiastical – and where are the Niebuhrs and the Temples of yester-year? This is the continuing yet constantly changing role of the church – with cues and leads being supplied from many highly conditioned times and places. Yet they are likely, I would guess, to come in future less from the old centres than the new edges – like liberation theology, black theology and women's theology. They will be heard too across the frontiers of other disciplines, other ideologies and other faiths. They will come not simply from above nor simply from below. They will arise out of that engagement to holy worldliness where those like monks and mystics who, in Bonhoeffer's distinction, live life from the inside out meet in creative encounter with that greater number of Christians who will always live it from the outside in. And the expression of this ethic will increasingly have to be worked out alongside those who are out of the church altogether but who are drawn together and driven on by what Christians would recognize as the vision and the claims of the kingdom and what Roger Garaudy, the French Marxist, has called 'the never satisfied exigency in man', which, he says, 'is the flesh of your God'.

VI

THE PLACE OF LAW IN THE FIELD OF SEX

This is a lecture (the Beckly Lecture on a Methodist foundation in the field of Christian social ethics, given in July 1972 and since brought up to date) which has a limited theme – albeit a vast one and one where as a non-lawyer I should properly fear to tread. But at least let me begin by delimiting its range. I am not here speaking on the place of moral law in relation to love: that I attempted to do in my *Christian Morals Today*, included in a revised form in my *Christian Freedom in a Permissive Society*. Rather I want to speak on the place of criminal law in relation to sex.

This, as I said, is a much more limited theme, but one nevertheless that tends quickly to spill over into wider and more diffuse areas. Thus, when we are confronted with something of which we deeply disapprove (especially if we have not thought deeply about it), there is an instinctive reaction to say, 'There ought to be a law against it.' But this is to equate the place of criminal law with that of moral condemnation. Clearly, once we do think about it, this simple equation cannot be sustained. That way leads to the regimentation of morals and the police state. Yet so pervasive is the assumption that if you do not approve of something (for instance, pornography) you must wish to prohibit it and, even more, that if you permit it you must therefore approve it, that it is desirable to begin by doing a bit of sorting out.

Let us then draw out the implications of the phrase, 'There ought to be a law against it'.

In the first place, the function of the law is primarily being seen as negative. We all know that you cannot (regretfully) make people good by Act of Parliament, but at least, it is argued, you can stop them straying too far. The function of law then is to keep them within the straight and narrow, to prohibit undesirable deviation. And this, of course, is the popular image of the officer of the law with his hob-nailed boots: 'Now then, now then! What's going on here?' If it isn't quite 'Find out what Johnnie's doing and tell him to stop it', it is something very near it. And the charge against the permissive society is that the controls have slipped: things are being permitted that ought not to be permitted.

And the second implication is that society or its leading members have the right to control, to say what shall be permitted. In all this talk there is a 'you' and a 'them' ('You cannot make people good, but. . .'). And the function of law in such a paternalistic understanding of society is by its sanctions to promote the values, to enforce the morality, of those who know best, whether this is an oligarchy of self-appointed guardians or what John Stuart Mill called 'the tyranny of the majority'. Its function, as he said, in this way of thinking, is that of 'moral police', to prescribe what it is good for us to read or think or do and to proscribe what it is not. In the vigorous words of Lord Mansfield in 1774, 'Whatever is *contra bonos mores et decorum* the principles of our laws prohibit, and the King's Court as the general censor and guardian of the public morals is bound to restrain and punish.' Originally this function covered (and in most countries of the world still covers) all areas dangerous to the unity or stability of society – religious (or ideological), political and moral. Indeed, as Lord Devlin put it in his classic presentation of this view, *The Enforcement of Morals*, 'the suppression of vice is as much the law's business as the suppression of subversive activities'. But, though we still have blasphemy (and of course security) laws on the statute book and though proponents of a radically alternative society are far from unharassed, it is, at any rate in peace-time in the United Kingdom (outside Ulster), only in the moral field, curiously narrowed down to the sexual, that the censor, the negative guardian, now operates. In fact when the real thrust of the attack is social or political (as was arguably the case in the *Oz* trial of 1971) the establishment is compelled to go in under the cover (only too liberally provided) of obscenity.

But I do not want to get involved at this point in the debate about censorship. I simply instance it as the one surviving feature still backed by the criminal code, as opposed to other social pressures, of the paternalistic concept of the function of law. According to this concept the place of law in the field of sex is potentially unlimited – as indeed one can see from the fact that still under the Sexual Offences Act of 1967 anal sex between husband and wife in the privacy of their bedroom is in theory punishable with life imprisonment. For this is the 'abominable crime' of buggery, and, quite consistently, if it is morally abominable it must legally be prohibited. But it is to America, the land of the free, that you must go for the full out-working of this theory. There, with the sole exception of New Mexico (where, as a late arrival to statehood, they evidently did not do their prep), every possible sexual activity with the exception of 'normal' conjugal union and solitary masturbation (and even in Indiana, the home ironically of the Kinsey Institute, the latter!) has been declared criminal in one state or another and usually in most. This applies to prostitution (in all states), adultery and even fornication. No doubt much of this is dead wood, though in Boston as late as 1954 the sex laws were reported to receive 'normal' enforcement, and in 1948 there were 248 arrests for adultery in that city. Indeed it has been estimated that, on the evidence of the Kinsey Report, 95% of the American people should have been in jail for sexual offences alone! But unenforced or unenforceable law is bad law; and if law is to be respected here or anywhere else it should be commendable on the ground that 'you *know* it makes sense'.

I have quoted these rather extreme instances not for the sake of presenting a *reductio ad absurdum* or of settling by ridicule what is a perfectly serious issue. I quote them because it becomes increasingly clear to me that if we are to have sexual laws that make sense it is not merely a question of trimming away dead wood, or the more absurd growths, but of looking again at the tree that was capable of producing such fruits. For they were entirely logical growths. If the function of law is the public enforcement of private morals, then if you *can* prohibit what you think is morally wrong or offensive, you should.

I wish to argue that this whole theory is fallacious and that we shall not get our sexual laws right until we can detach ourselves from it and start again. But I am well aware that there is a powerful emotional investment in this theory amongst 'right thinking' people (in both senses); and this is increased if, like me, they are middle-class and middle-aged. The temptation, if you see something you abominate, to reach for the gun of prohibition is almost irresistible. But it is a sobering thought (if that is the right word) that this is also what the great American people tried to do in the twenties with

Prohibition with a big 'P'. The effects of prohibition, as of all forms of censorship, can be notoriously counter-productive. Like other forms of authorized violence (such as internment without trial or the resort to criminal sanctions in industrial conflict), it can merely feed the problem rather than solve it. Nevertheless, I find it difficult to convince people that it is precisely because I am against pornography that I want (with the conditions I shall mention later) to permit it rather than prohibit it. Yet I assume that there would be very few, however much they oppose alcohol, or for that matter smoking, who would think the sensible way to achieve their end was to make it illegal. Similarly the last thing the Josephine Butler Society has wanted in its fight against prostitution is that it should be made into a crime.

All this is partly a matter of thinking through the issue far enough to see the consequences. Hence it is those who have thought most about capital punishment or suicide or homosexuality or obscenity (instead of relying, with Mr Nixon, on 'centuries of civilization and ten minutes of common sense') who have tended to come out on the side of loosening rather than tightening the law – including, impressively, the American Presidential Commission on Obscenity and Pornography, whose 640-page Report (however one may dispute its judgment) cannot be accused of skipping its homework. But it is also, more importantly, a matter of recognizing that *the function of law in society is not to prohibit but to protect, not to enforce morals but to safeguard persons, their privacies and freedoms.*

This, of course, is no new doctrine. It received its classic and oft-quoted expression in John Stuart Mill's essay *On Liberty*:

> The only purpose for which power can rightfully be exercised over any member of a civilized community, against his will, is to prevent harm to others.

He indeed stressed the last two words 'to others' with a devotion to *laissez faire* that strikes us in a socialized society as magnificent but quixotic:

> His own good, either physical or moral, is not a sufficient warrant. He cannot rightfully be compelled to do or forbear because it will be better for him to do so, because it will make him happier, because, in the opinions of others, to do so would be wise, or even right.

It would seem to most of us that society has the right, and indeed the duty, to protect the individual against himself in the matter, say, of provenly noxious drugs (if only because in the complexity of modern life the individual is usually in no position to assess the danger, and to prevent him becoming a liability upon the community). The same applies to that last bulwark of Tory freedom (still doggedly defended by the House of Lords) – the refusal to legislate for the compulsory wearing of seat-belts: it is the rest of us who are left to pick up the bits – and the bill. Nevertheless, in a country where suicide is no longer a crime, while aiding and abetting it is, Mill's distinction cannot be dismissed. Moreover, a man can be so protected against himself (particularly morally) that he ceases to be free (and therefore capable of morality).

But on the main issue, however difficult we may find it, like Mill, to be wholly consistent, I am convinced that he was vitally correct. The function of criminal law and 'the only purpose for which power can rightfully be exercised over any member of a civilized community against his will' is the positive one of preventing harm to others. This may, of course, *involve* prohibition or restriction – effective gun-laws are an obvious case in point – but the *raison d'être* of the law is protection, not prohibition. *And where there is no need for protection it should not intervene.* It is not there to express what Charles Davis has called 'the anger of morality', however 'abominable' may be the object of its disapprobation. It is there as far as possible to *enable* people to be free, mature, adult human beings, or what the New Testament calls 'sons'. Of course, it cannot *make* people sons. But it has a role, a limited role, in hindering the hindrances. It is limited because the free processes of influence, education, example and persuasion are so much more productive. But as a last resort if a person refuses to respect the freedom of another there must be provision to compel him to do so.

With this as a principle I should like to look specifically at the field of sexual law – though if we could abolish the 'sexual offence' as we have abolished the 'marital offence' there would, I believe, be a great gain in perspective. For it is the *person* – not his sexuality – that the law is there to protect. And many sexual offences are relatively minor as 'assaults' (often involving no violence) but are blown up out of all proportion by being labelled 'indecent'. The 'sex offender' finds himself branded for life. If such trespasses upon the liberty of others could be subsumed under 'offences against the person' this might be a real step in the direction of eliminating the peculiar vindictiveness which our society – sometimes represented by the magistrate – reserves for sexual aberrations and deviations.

Within the sexual area one could take as a starting-point the statement of the 1957 Report of the Wolfenden Committee on Homosexual Offences and Prostitution, which, as Professor Hart has pointed out in his reply to Lord Devlin, *Law, Liberty and Morality*, is strikingly similar to the principle enunciated by Mill. The function of criminal law, it says,

> is to preserve public order and decency, to protect the citizen from what is offensive or injurious, and to provide sufficient safeguards against exploitation or corruption of others, particularly those who are specially vulnerable because they are young, weak in body or mind, inexperienced, or in a state of special physical, official or economic dependence.

On this basis the Committee proceeded to ground its recommendations to obviate the offensive public manifestations of prostitution (though not to make it illegal) and to remove from the area of criminality homosexual acts between 'consenting adults in private'. This last, now famous, phrase provides in fact a convenient three-sided boundary to what the Report described as that 'realm of private morality and immorality which is, in brief and crude terms, not the law's business'. *Per contra* we can use it as a guide to where the law has a right and a duty to protect the citizen – that is to say:

1. Where there is not true consent;
2. Where there is not adult responsibility;
3. Where there is obtrusion on the public.

Let us consider each of these in turn, and we shall find that they get progressively more difficult to determine.

1. The first presents relatively little trouble, though consent is clearly a matter of degree, especially among those of diminished responsibility or in a state of 'physical, official or economic dependence'. Offences against consent would obviously include rape, enticement, deception, blackmail, and some (but not all) forms of prostitution – however much all forms of prostitution (and for that matter some marriages) may be judged morally, though not legally, exploitative. But if an adult freely and knowingly consents to sell himself or herself for sexual purposes then the law has no right to intervene, though here as elsewhere it can properly protect against abuse the conditions of the market. But although this first condition is relatively simple, it is fundamental to the preservation of persons as persons. Each of the others must presuppose it as essential.

2. The second condition raises the question, 'What is the age of consent?', or, 'Who is a responsible adult?' One perfectly true an-

swer to the latter might be, 'None of us is.' But clearly this cannot be taken as the basis of legal definition. Ideally, too, and more convincingly, one could argue that there should be no fixed age of consent. Wherever you draw the line, especially at the variable, and changing, age of puberty, it is bound to be arbitrary; therefore each case must be judged on its merits. But obviously an adult before having sexual relations with a boy or girl must know in advance whether he or she is breaking the law: it is no protection for a judge afterwards to opine that the young person was not old enough to give consent. A line must be drawn, however arbitrarily.

But a line for what? Under English law a person is deemed legally to be capable of different things at varying ages – for instance, of committing rape at 14, or getting married at 16, of voting and jury service (and therefore of judging such cases) at 18, of homosexual relations (if a man) at 21. In this connection, we are dealing not with the age at which we think young people *morally should* have sex relations, but with the age at which they *legally can* consent to what they are doing. And this is potentially lower than for marriage, which involves heavier commitments and responsibilities.

Two things can, I think, be said straight away. First, the age for homosexual and heterosexual relations ought to be the same, since it is capacity for personal consent which is at issue and not sexual proclivity – unless, of course, one applied the previous argument and said that since heterosexual relationships imply the possible procreation of children the age of responsibility for them should be higher. Second, the present age of consent for male homosexual relationships is absurdly high. It was fixed at a time when the age of majority in general was 21, though even then the evidence presented to the Wolfenden Committee by the Church of England Moral Welfare Council recommended an age of consent of 17 for both sexes. Since female homosexual relationships have never been illegal no age of consent for them has been defined. Yet as the 1979 Working Paper on the Age of Consent in relation to Sexual Offences produced by the Home Office Policy Advisory Committee on Sexual Offences points out, 'section 14 of the Sexual Offences Act 1956 (indecent assault on a woman) effectively provides an age of consent of 16 for them, since a girl under the age of 16 cannot in law give consent which would prevent an act being an assault for the purposes of the section.'

I suggest therefore that we start from the proposition that the legal age of consent for all sex relationships should be 16. This was powerfully argued in the minority report, entirely written incidentally by women members, of the Working Paper just referred to. (The majority accepted the lowering of homosexual consent to 18.) Indeed I believe the only real argument is whether or not it should be lower than 16. For two things follow from the age of consent: (*a*) Below it liability for criminal prosecution automatically arises, and few would want to see a teen-aged boy sent to jail for fathering the child of a 15-year old he intends to marry (as I gather can actually happen in permissive Denmark, where a girl under age is legally required to state the name of the father and thus expose him to prosecution!). (*b*) It is, technically, aiding and abetting a criminal offence to prescribe contraceptives for those below the age of consent. In practice if this is done in good faith the doctor or social worker involved will not be prosecuted. But legally one is still in a very grey area. To be compelled to break or ignore the law in order to protect them and their potential unborn babies is an unnecessarily heavy responsibility and merely helps to bring the law into disrepute. The added fear of criminal proceedings also of course deters the young from seeking advice.

I do not find it easy to make up my mind on this issue. On the one hand, there is no doubt that the line drawn by the law does have a deterrent effect and protects children of school age who might otherwise be exposed to relationships for which they are not ready and responsibilities which they are in no position to carry. Yet the criminal law is a very blunt instrument for this purpose and is in danger of being discredited if it is not implemented, or even respected, except in particularly blatant cases. Three comments will serve to bring this out.

The first is from Lord Devlin, the great protagonist of the view that the law's job is 'the enforcement of morals'. Remarking on such court cases, he said this: 'The object of the law, as judges repeatedly tell juries, is to protect young girls against themselves; but juries are not impressed.' In other words, the layman knows perfectly well that in all too many cases the law does not correspond to realities. And this is bad for the law. It is not simply that it is good law disobeyed; it is unrealistic law not respected.

And the same point comes through the second comment, this time from a woman doctor who is also a deaconess of the Church of England: 'I break the law regularly on the matter of advice to young people and both the girls and I find that this is absurd, and difficult. I also have sympathy with men who find themselves in court.'

The third comes from a specialist social worker on the other side of the argument, who believes that the real offenders are getting off far too lightly. In an analysis of 40 cases of illegal sexual intercourse with girls under 16 known personally to her, no action was taken in 31 cases. In the majority of these she agreed that action was either undesirable or impossible. But the cases she detailed fell without exception into the kind for which I shall argue there should be increased protection (either because of lack of consent, mental retardation, or the need for care and protection). What is happening at the moment is that people are not being protected who should be protected, because the law is too undiscriminating an instrument to be pressed home.

The issue is *how* most effectively to protect the young. Is it by declaring all early teen-age sex illegal and then turning a blind eye? Would it not be more honest and constructive to remove the fiction that all such persons are (by definition) indulging in criminal activity and then substitute effective and selective protection under the Children and Young Persons Act for those whose immaturity really is being exploited by older men (or women)? In fact an age, or ages, of protection would seem to be a more relevant category than one of consent. Consent is too personal and subjective to be determined by an arbitrary age. But there must be a line or lines below which society has a duty to assume responsibility for protecting the immature. I would throw out the proposal that the lower line should be 14, so that no one having intercourse with a person above that age should automatically be committing a criminal offence, but that between 14 and 17 care and protection proceedings (with their dual criteria of admitted offence and need) would be available for those who really were being exploited or corrupted, as Wolfenden put it, through their inexperience.

But here, as elsewhere, the place of law is a limited one. Indeed, to introduce its scrutinies and its sanctions may often do more harm than good. Speaking of the effect of sexual experience on children, a former probation officer, Mr John Nicholson, has said this in a letter from which he has allowed me to quote:

> 'Harm' results much more from the tension between an individual's experience and that of his reference-group than from the experience in itself. Some research on childhood 'victims' of sexual offences would appear to bear this out in that it is the subsequent parental horror, police investigation, etc., which are significantly more disturbing than the offence. Consequently the best protection we can afford children is the extension of what

experience or behaviour we can embrace, survive and ultimately be enriched by. Vis-à-vis *this* concept of protection I think law may well need to have a declaratory and educative function as well as merely a constraining one.

These are wise words, with broader application.

Finally, under this second condition of adult responsibility, it is clearly possible and desirable to include special protection of the young in any regulations made on the subject of censorship, film classifications, television timings, etc. But this issue of censorship and control brings us to the third and even more contentious line, that between private and public.

3. As the Wolfenden Report recognized, the point at which it becomes the law's business to intervene is when the legitimate privacy of the individual requires protection against intrusion. This cuts both ways. First, the individual requires protection against the police, the press, informers, blackmailers, etc., bringing into the public realm what is essentially his private affair. But, equally, the individual member of the public can expect protection against having forced upon him through hoardings, advertisements, window-displays, unsolicited mailings, public entertainments and the mass-media what invades his privacy by being, in the etymological sense of the words, 'indecent' or 'obscene', that is, inappropriate to the time or place or (if this is the ultimate derivation of obscenity) having presented on stage what should be off.

Let us consider each of these aspects of privacy.

Under the first there is still a good deal of tidying up of the law to be done, especially in bringing legislation (and its implementation) into line for heterosexual and homosexual relationships. The definition of privacy for homosexuals (if male) is still much more restricted than it is for heterosexuals. They cannot with security show the usual signs of affection in public, and even in a private house no other person may be present during homosexual relations. As the House of Lords judgment on the *International Times* case of 1972 established, they may not use the press to make contact with one another for non-criminal purposes – a liberty not, as far as I know, denied to any other of Her Majesty's subjects. And this, of course, threatens the freedom also of those in the churches or elsewhere who seek to promote social facilities and support-groups for them and generally to help the lonely break out of their isolation and establish regular relationships.

As a positive principle one might say that any discrimination between the sexes, here as elsewhere, should itself be made illegal. And this goes also for the inequality of penalties (e.g., for indecent assault on a man – ten years; for indecent assault on a woman – two years). Penalties for homosexual offences were actually increased (partly under ecclesiastical pressure) beyond the recommendation of the Wolfenden Report as a condition of its acceptance, and they have added to the jungle of anomalies in this field arising from piecemeal sexual legislation and uncoordinated by-laws. There is still no consent or privacy at all guaranteed under the law for male homosexuals in Northern Ireland, the armed services or the merchant navy, and under the Armed Services Acts consensual homosexual acts in private remain a breach of discipline whether or not they are committed on duty or on services premises. Moreover, the implementation of the Act remains disconcertingly uneven, with varying police policies and unpredictable interpretations of such vague concepts as a 'breach of the peace' or 'insulting behaviour'. It should surely be accepted that homosexuals should be harassed and prosecutions initiated only when public decency is palpably outraged or actual annoyance is caused to specific persons.

Above all the law dealing with under-age homosexual behaviour differs radically from legislation on heterosexual age of consent, in making the under-age partner a criminal offender as well as the one who is over 21. This cannot by any stretch of the imagination be justified as 'protective'. Indeed as the Home Office Advisory Committee on Sexual Offences itself says of heterosexual relations,

> A girl under 16 cannot be convicted of an offence when she has sexual intercourse with a man. . . . The Court for Crown Cases Reserved [has] said that it would be incompatible with the protective aim of the law if a girl could be convicted as aider and abetter of the man in those circumstances.

Here is a clear point of discrimination where the law must surely be revised.

Finally, under this heading of safeguarding civil liberties, careful attention needs to be paid to the law regarding 'incitement', under which a person can be prosecuted for encouraging others to do something which is not unlawful but which, as Sir Peter Rawlinson, the then Solicitor General, put it in Parliament on 7 July 1964, 'might be said to be immoral', and to the recourse by the judiciary to common law charges, especially the vague and oppressive charge, first invoked in 1960 and still embodied in no legislation, of 'conspiracy to corrupt public morals'. According to Lord Reid's concurring judgement in the *International Times* case, in which the latter was most notoriously used, there have been 'at least thirty and probably more convictions of this crime in the ten years that have elapsed' since its invocation. As Bernard Levin powerfully pleaded in *The Times* of 20 and 22 June 1972, this is one of the areas calling for urgent clarification and parliamentary redress. Indeed, as the law stands at the moment, *no* homosexual behaviour, including that between consenting adults in private, is fully *lawful* even though it is not criminal. This is because of the presumption that all sexual intercourse outside marriage is *contra bonos mores* and therefore 'unlawful'. This presumption is archaic, unenforceable, and in its social consequences far-reaching and frequently harmful. It should specifically be reversed.

Since the *International Times* case related to obscenity and public decency, it brings us to the other part of this section, namely, the protection of members of the public against having *their* privacies invaded or susceptibilities offended.

In approaching the complex issues of censorship, on which I wrote more fully in my article 'Obscenity and Maturity' in *Christian Freedom in a Permissive Society*, let me first restate the general principle that it is not the job of the law to try to make people pure or stop them being prurient – though it has frequently attempted the latter. The function of any kind of legal restriction is not the enforcement of a code of morality or a standard of taste, whether it be of the majority or of a minority that knows best, but the protection of freedoms, whether again of the majority or of a minority. Specifically in regard to sexual obscenity one could say that *the aim of the law should be not to prohibit those who want pornography* (which is largely what it has bent its energies to doing) *but to protect those who don't.* In private, persons should be free and protected to read or see what they like – even if others dislike or disapprove of it intensely. In public, persons must be free and protected, within limits, from having forced upon them what they find indecent or objectionable. I say 'within limits', firstly, because persons can, again, be so protected that they cease to be free; secondly, because there is a severe limit to what can be enforced by law, and a law which is unenforceable is bad law; and, thirdly, because any restriction is a limitation of someone else's freedom and is justifiable only if, in the words of a 1972 report, *The Pollution of the Mind*, from the Society of Conservative Lawyers, the material is 'grossly offensive to the public at large'.

Since then there has appeared in 1979 the Home Office Report of the Committee on Obscenity and Film Censorship chaired by Bernard Williams. This represents a sustained, readable and cogent case for the sort of position I have been urging. Apart from prohibiting live sex-performances and pictures and films which involve persons under 16 or the infliction of actual physical harm, it recommends protecting adults solely by the restriction to clearly designated premises of matter whose *unrestricted availability is offensive to reasonable people*. This means that those who wish to see it can, while those who do not are relieved from having it forced on them. The Report recommends no restriction on the printed word; and this is probably wise, since one could then expect that the purely 'dirty book' of no literary merit would gravitate towards its natural outlets and be the more readily declined by regular book-sellers.

Indeed it would in general be easier to draw the line of acceptability higher if other openings were available. If people have the freedom to see or do what they like as long as they are not disturbing others, then one can be a good deal tougher in enforcing the limits than if what is objectionable to the majority is suppressed altogether. Moreover, there are many things about sex which are in no way obscene in themselves and don't have to be defined as such (indeed the Christian must assert that the erotic is positively good) but which can reasonably be objected to if paraded or placarded in public. Sex is essentially an intimate area of life and to have it foisted upon one on any or every occasion is an unwarrantable intrusion. Privacies must be respected and protected. But the corollary is that there should be freedom where no one is compelled to share it.

Let me draw out the point with an analogy. I dislike *having* to breathe in tobacco smoke. I would not go as far as James I in his *Counterblast to Tobacco* in describing smoking as 'a custom loathsome to the eye, hateful to the nose, harmful to the brain, dangerous to the lungs, and in the black stinking fume thereof nearest resembling the horrible Stygian smoke of the pit that is bottomless'. Let me merely say that I prefer when travelling to look out a non-smoking compartment. But when I have sat in one and someone starts lighting up, I am adamant; and I find myself assuming the role of law-enforcement officer as I seldom would elsewhere. Yet I can be firm only because I know there is another compartment along the corridor to which he can perfectly well go and indulge his pollution to his heart's content. The last thing I wish to do is to ban smoking or start prosecutions against it. Such procedures would merely make even more people want to smoke.

I would take the same line with regard to the so-called 'pollution of the mind'. I think it is noxious and thoroughly uninviting, and I don't want to have to breathe it. The real charge against pornography, in all, what the Williams Report calls its 'tastelessness and depressing awfulness', is that it is *anti*-erotic – destructive of what God saw and behold it was very good. Fortunately, however, satiety sets in a good deal sooner than it does with either tobacco or alcohol. When you have seen the lot, you've seen the lot; and, as the American Presidential Report showed, there is a law of rapidly diminishing returns. I would prefer to speak of hard-bore rather than hard-core. The amount of actual damage it does is certainly a good deal less than that of either of the two legalized commodities I have mentioned. This is not to say that its effect is negligible or that pornography does no harm, and, as with tobacco and alcohol, we must protect (especially the young) against the *abuse* of sex where we can. But the damage is paradoxically probably the opposite of what most people seem to fear. It is not the heightening or intensifying of the drive that is likely to result from a distorted sexual environment so much as its crippling and constricting. This is even more true of the effect of destructive personal *relationships* – one bad encounter may permanently impair a person's sexual development. But you cannot ultimately protect against these by law. And distorted books and pictures about sex are likely to have attraction in the long term only for those whose sex-*relations* have been a failure. In other words, pornography appeals *in an enslaving or addictive way* only to those who, for reasons that go much further back into childhood and adolescence, are sexually sick or lonely. They are depraved because they are deprived, and should be pitied rather than prosecuted – and above all helped. In so far as pornography, like excessive smoking or drinking, is a symptom of a sick society, let us apply all the cures and dissuasives we know. But censoring the symptoms is not only useless but counter-productive. For Freud should have taught us that our repressed impulses are often far more violent *because* they are repressed than they would be if they were allowed expression.

And this is fully borne out in the field of sexual legislation by the experience of Denmark. Although, unlike other pilgrims, I was there for quite different purposes (lecturing, in fact, on the New Testament), I took the opportunity, as chairman of the Sexual Law Reform Society, to talk to a number of people, almost all of them Christians, about their reactions to the abolition of censorship. *No one* I talked to had any wish to go back on this, and the kind of backlash and moral crusading we have in Britain was apparently negligible. For the legal changes had been put through (incidentally by a Conservative administration) not in order to satisfy a lust for licence but precisely, as I have been advocating, to protect public decency against invasions of privacy. As long as the only weapon for securing this was the blunt one of suppressing 'obscenity' the law was becoming a laughing-stock. For, as everyone has found at the end of the road, an objective definition of obscenity is legally impossible, and prosecutions whether successful or unsuccessful merely stimulate the demand. Now, by allowing people to read or see anything in private, the heat has been taken off, and what is public is a good deal cleaner in every way (which would not be difficult) than in many English cities. The Danes do not appear to suffer from what D. H. Lawrence called 'sex in the head', and after the first much-publicized flush the surviving sex-shops and live shows (the latter of which have never been *public* entertainments and have now in fact all been closed) are largely kept going by the tourist trade.

My overall impression was very much borne out by that left later on the Williams Committee:

> It was clear that the whole subject was of very little interest to the officials and police officers to whom we spoke in Denmark, and this in turn is because the population at large finds very little controversy in the present situation. There seems to be no significant lobby for a return the laws prohibiting pornography. There are some groups campaigning against moral decline, but pornography is not a central issue for them and we found a recognition among them that fresh measures against pornography would not command significant support in the Danish Parliament. The clear impression which emerges is that for the Danes the crime of pornography is now dead.

Just as New Mexico, for all its absence of immorality laws, is apparently no more libidinous than any other American state, so the abolition of censorship in Denmark does not promote lewdness or growth in sexual crime, rather, if anything, the opposite. There is indeed some correlation between the availability of pornography and a decline in sex-crimes, notably against children, which is carefully assessed by the Williams Committee. In fact the last thing a far-sighted peddler of pornography should want, if he knows which side his bread is buttered, is the legalization of complete sexual freedom. Even Soho can see that far. The rumour that

Scotland Yard, under its then new Commissioner, Robert Mark, intended to act merely on complaints from the public in place of a seek-and-destroy policy was not exactly received with elation by the book-shop managers. According to a *Sunday Times* report of 30 April 1972, one pessimist frankly admitted that he expected legalized porn to follow – with 'the catastrophic drop in prices that would mean'.

This sounds so paradoxical and to most people such rot that the logic behind it needs spelling out further. Indeed there is concealed here a perfectly intelligent objection, and intelligible fear, namely that to legalize is *ipso facto* to license. One of the main functions of the law, it is said, is to 'set a good example'. What is lawful is what society approves: to make lawful what has hitherto been unlawful is equivalent to giving it the stamp of social approbation. It is a way of saying, 'You have said that I can.'

Now there is an area where this logic applies. A de-restriction sign on the roadside says precisely this. Of course, it does not say that you *should* immediately drive at top speed, but it says that you can. This however is because we are here dealing with a department of life that for reasons of safety has to be fully regulated by law. But mercifully this is not true of all life, or we should be living in a society where, as was said of the Kaiser's Germany, everything was compulsory that was not *verboten*. In most areas of living there is a wide margin of tolerance – and the more mature the society the wider it will be – where the individual is free to make moral choices without the law being involved. And to de-restrict something legally does not imply that it is morally to be encouraged. Such a step may merely be an acknowledgement that the law has been an ass or has ceased to correspond with social realities. Thus, to remove suicide from being a criminal offence is not to set society's seal of approval upon it. And there is no reason to suppose that more people now attempt suicide *because* it is legal and therefore 'all right'. If they do, it is because modern life has greater strains. To reimpose the law would lessen none of them, merely add to them. Equally, the suppression of homosexuality by law solves nothing. To free it (in situations where others are not forced or offended) is not to promote it. Rather it is to remove fear and to afford the facilities for coping constructively with the issues it raises.

In actual fact the force of law as a power for good in these areas is a good deal weaker than we tend to suppose. It is not the law that alters social attitudes so much as social attitudes the law. It is not because the law has changed – it hasn't – that more illegally conceived (and not merely illegitimate) babies are being born to girls under 16. It is because of a change of social mores and the half-arrival of contraceptives. To stiffen the law would not staunch the flow: it would merely make advice and protection more difficult.

Yet people have a deep-seated fear that if you lift the legal controls anything could happen and probably would. There is a catastrophic expectation of unlimited indulgence. For a time, no doubt, with pornography there would be a private boom – though in public things might be a good deal better. But social controls, quite apart from what people actually *want* to read and see, would by the usual checks and balances soon reassert themselves. The notion that 'anything goes' just because the law allows it reflects the paternalistic assumption that it is the function of law to tell people what is good for them and that what is not prohibited is thereby promoted. But it is precisely a sign of a civilized society that it progressively substitutes the free processes of social judgment for the sanctions of penal suppression.

In this lecture, I would stress again, I have been concerned with the place and the role of criminal law. This does not in the least mean that other pressures and educative processes have not a vital, and indeed an increasing, function. The publicity campaign against smoking, albeit conducted with one arm tied behind the back by commercial – and budgetary – interests, is an example of what can be mounted. In this campaign law has a perfectly valid place in enforcing warnings and controlling advertisement: not taking away people's freedoms, but respecting and instructing them. We are not shut up to a choice of prohibition *or* indifferentism. Indeed, if we could let the law mind its own business, the field would be freer for other forms of social suasion, voluntary self-discipline and professional restraint. At present we do little because we are led to suppose that the only available action is legal action – which every time there is an obscenity trial (whatever the outcome) merely inflates the problem. How many, for instance, in this country would ever have heard of *Last Exit to Brooklyn*, let alone toiled with its turgidities, if it had not been for the misguided zeal of Sir Cyril Black? There are so many more intelligent ways of doing good.

Yet let me in closing re-emphasize the positive, and quite indispensable, function of law in the sexual field. It is to protect the assaulted, the young and feeble-minded, and to guard the privacies of the individual, whether in private or in public. If we can reform it to do that effectively and constructively in a manner that commands consent and therefore respect, we shall have done a great thing. For the rest, the way is open, now more than ever, for the immense corporate task laid upon all of us of helping to transform ourselves from a paternalistic society, through the adolescent pains and follies of a permissive society, *towards* a more genuinely mature society.

This of course does not mean a society consisting of totally secure people. There are, and always will be, persons in need of special care and protection, immature adults, neurotic adults and dangerous psychopaths. What matters is our direction and our aim. And for a statement of that I cannot do better than end with a quotation from Dr Faith Spicer, medical director of the London Youth Advisory Service, whose concern for the whole person in the field of sexual counselling is an example to us all. In her book, *Sex and the Love Relationship*, she writes this:

> I hope we are a shade more honest, a shade more compassionate. I hope we gradually, by learning *why* people behave as they do, will learn to help them, and how to prevent the early damage that may be responsible for their actions, so that . . . we can at least have a society in which we know whom to protect, and in what way to protect them, so that the rest can feel free to trust their own judgment, and find their own way to a real and lasting love relationship.

VII

CHRISTIANS AND VIOLENCE

I start from a verse of scripture, not because I know what it means, but because I don't. It is the enigmatic words of Matt. 11.12, rendered in the NEB: 'Ever since the coming of John the Baptist the kingdom of Heaven has been subjected to violence and violent men are seizing it.' But in the margin there is a very different translation: 'Ever since the coming of John the Baptist the kingdom of Heaven has been forcing its way forward, and men of force are seizing it.' In the first the violence or force is a bad thing, in the second it is a good thing. In St Matthew's context I suspect the first translation is correct. But in his parallel, but different, version Luke (16.16) supports the second.

I begin in this way because it illustrates the ambiguity of violence. It would be easy to say of violence, as of the preacher about sin, simply that 'he was against it'. Indeed I am instinctively and passionately against it. Violence has no attraction for me whatever either in real life or on the screen, and I have selected this subject because I knew it would be good for me to have to face it. For it is too easy just to shy away from it.

Sex – violence – death. It is not for nothing that violence forms the middle term in what looks like a rakes' progress. Sex and violence are often twinned – and rightly so because there are deep and dark undercurrents here associated with the life-force. Yet they are not identical twins. For the one basically is creative of life, the other destructive. And of the two the pornography of violence is, I have no doubt, far the more dangerous. Equally, violence and death walk hand in hand. In the growing spate of hi-jacking and hostages, in the seemingly endless agony of Palestine and Northern Ireland, in the battering of babies and the systematic use of torture, in the mindless muggings and gratuitous vandalism of our age, the connection between them is only too sickeningly obvious.

Yet again I would insist that violence is disconcertingly ambiguous. The 'vi' part of it comes ultimately from the same root as 'vitality'. And behind that lies the even closer association in the Greek between *bios*, life, and *bia*, violence.

There is the same ambiguity too about those other terrible twins in the name of which violence is opposed: 'law and order'. Ostensibly they are the pillars of virtue. But order without justice is an expression of violence, whether against the person or the group. One could illustrate this from the economic order or the political or the psychological, from Russia or Chile, Southern Africa or North-East Brazil. Indeed Helder Camara has written out of the experience of the last of what he calls 'the spiral of violence'. What he styles 'violence no. 1' is the institutionalized violence of built-in injustice. And it is the most difficult form of violence for middle-class or white people to recognize as violence at all. For it manifests itself precisely not in disorder but in order, the imposed order of oppression. And this is the root-cause of 'violence no. 2', the violence of protest and resistance, of freedom-fighters or terrorists, according to the way you look at them. And that leads equally inexorably to 'violence no. 3' – the repression by the forces of law and order, again whether this is viewed as protective or invasive. Then the cycle starts again, with the life-sentences and the death-chants, the threats of reprisal and the rest, and the cry goes up, 'How long, O Lord?'

But finally, before we turn to our attitude towards it, a word more on the causes of violence. It is so easy to moralize the problem, and see violence primarily as a symptom of wickedness. But it is just as much a symptom of structures, whether of society or the psyche. We all know what happens if you merely increase the number of rats in a cage. There is a thin threshold between viability and violence. And the frictions of family or housing, the polarizations of poverty or colour, can be as destructive as the pressures of population. If we are moving into an increasingly violent society, where few of us can escape being *to some extent* battered or schizophrenic, it is no good just preaching love and the liberal values. As Reinhold Niebuhr said many years ago in his *Interpretation of Christian Ethics*:

The health of a social organism depends upon the adequacy of

> its social structure as much as does the health of the body upon the biochemical processes. No degree of goodwill alone can cure a deficiency in glandular secretions; and no moral idealism can overcome a basic mechanical defect in the social structure.

That is why attention to 'violence no. 1' is of primal importance, not merely economically and politically but psycho-socially. Yet how much money or care do we put into such areas of disaffection – until they explode? We are always finding ourselves reacting to violence – and by then the only alternative is apparently more violence. Procrastination, the hope that it will 'last my time', let alone Ian Smith's 'thousand years', with its endlessly repeated syndrome of too few concessions too late, is arguably the greatest occasion of violence in the modern world. Constantly as one went round South Africa – or Israel – one was haunted by John F. Kennedy's remark: 'It is those who make the peaceful revolution impossible who make the violent revolution inevitable.' And the blow-up there will be as nothing if we do not heed by measures of quite exceptional imaginativeness the implications of the Brandt Report on the economic imbalance of North and South, which is every whit as fateful as the more visible political tensions of East and West.

But enough of analysis. Let me sum up so far. The 'vi- factor', if I may coin the phrase, is an integral part of the natural order 'in Adam' – both for life and for death. In theological terms, it is God-given yet fallen. And it is not just going to go away by saying 'If only. . .'. The Bible itself is full of it. And so, if we are honest, are we all. Is there anyone who does not respond with one part of him to the superb vindictiveness, say, of the Song of Deborah and Barak in Judges 5? Much of the greatest human art has been the poetry, the painting, the theatre, of violence.

Yet, according to the gospel, we are not only in Adam but in Christ. What then is the distinctively Christian attitude to violence? Certainly it is not one of wishful thinking. As Isaac Watts said,

> When I survey the wondrous cross,
> Where the young prince of glory died. . .,

the sight is not a pretty one:

> His dying crimson, like a robe,
> Spreads o'er his body on the tree.

Editors have excised the 'young' and omitted or starred the latter verse. But they cannot finally censor the fact that Christianity, like no other religion, sets a Francis Bacon-like picture at the centre of its faith, in a way that is a stumbling-block to Muslims (whose Koran denies that Jesus really died) and a foolishness to Buddhists. Christianity is the religion of violence – transfigured. It is the way of crucified love, of a man of blood despoiling the powers and triumphing over them – not merely by non-violent resistance but by no resistance, in fact by proffering the *other* cheek (Matt. 5.38–48).

Yet absolute pacifism as a political programme is as simplistic as those offered by the law-and-order lobby or the sex-and-violence censors. For Jesus's words about non-resistance relate to suffering inflicted upon, evil done to, ourselves not other people. And this makes a vital difference. Suppose the Good Samaritan had arrived on the scene while the robbers were still beating up the wretched traveller. Should he not have resisted the evil? Should *he* have passed by on the other side? Here are some words of the New Testament scholar, John Knox:

> Jesus said: 'If a man smite you on one cheek turn the other also.' Here the situation is relatively simple – you and your enemy. But Jesus did not say: 'If any man smite one of your friends, lead him to another friend that he may smite *him* also.' Not only is it clear that Jesus could have made no such statement, but also that he would have felt that the involvement of the interests of others . . . transformed the whole moral situation and placed our obligations with respect to it in a radically different light.

I suspect that in fact we have subtly reversed Jesus's teaching. *Of course* when it is a matter of self-defence force is justified. No one would dream of calling us un-Christian if we coshed the burglar who coshed us. But if the World Council of Churches offers relief (*not* arms) to liberation movements in conditions such as we can hardly imagine and where every political solution is blocked, then Christians rise up to protest and distance themselves in righteous indignation.

There is much confusion here, and not a little hypocrisy. I am not a pacifist, nor are the majority of churchmen. I do not remember English Christians suggesting that the French resistance movement in the war against Hitler should never commit acts of sabotage. But I am absolutely convinced that non-violent resistance to injustice or oppression *whenever it is not entirely ruled out* is infinitely the better and more Christian way, even if it involves much more discipline, endurance and perhaps suffering. Yet it is the people in the situation who have ultimately to make their own choice of what ways are open and possible to them, whether it be the Maquis in France, the Patriotic Front in Rhodesia, Camillo Torres in Bolivia, or Martin Luther King in the States. It would be utterly wrong, as the World Council of Churches has made quite clear, to use Christian money to subsidize violence on either side. But it would be no less wrong not to fight oppression and injustice by every *other* available means. Do we really believe this as Christians? The resistance and inertia to such proposals to be encountered at every level in the councils of the church hardly suggests it. But if we do not believe it, at least do not let us use Jesus's words about non-resistance to evil as the ground for our inaction.

Yet these words, and still more the cross on which they were spelt out, *are* the clue to all our action (and suffering) in this matter – if we can receive them. Yet they are starting to make sense to more and more ordinary people in our power-crazy, power-hungry world. As Monica Furlong has written,

> The preaching of vulnerability, of gentleness, of detachment, of treating our brother as if he is Christ himself (or as our own self), and the insistence that it is the unlikely route that leads to happiness and fulfilment, has a kind of Alice in Wonderland perverseness about it, a perverseness so like life itself, that it has helped to persuade many of its essential truth.

There is finally no arguing about this: either you see it or you do not. But being a Christian in relation to violence is allowing that blinding insight, gradually or suddenly, to flood everything else, until we say again with Watts:

> Then am I dead to all the globe
> And all the globe is dead to me.

VIII

NUCLEAR POWER OPTIONS

I have hesitated over whether to include this chapter more than over any other. This is not because I do not think it important. On the contrary, the decisions on nuclear energy, coupled with the still more crucial and closely connected ones on nuclear warfare, which I have simply here had to leave untouched, are far more important for the sort of society we want, and indeed for our very survival, than anything relating to sex or violence. It is rather because they are so vital and so complex that as a non-scientist one hesitates to utter at all. Here more than anywhere factual details and technical judgments are inextricably involved in the moral and spiritual decisions – if, that is, the Word is really to be made flesh and mere moralizing is to be avoided. Moreover they are constantly shifting, and whatever one writes in this area is quickly in danger of being dated. But it becomes increasingly obvious that the issues are far too important to be left to the specialist, let alone to the nuclear establishment – which enjoys the advantage of enormous government resources not only for research and development but for channelling the information it chooses to purvey (or deny) to the public.

For the layman to enter this field is an education in itself, if only in picking one's path through the jungle of acronyms. I found myself going for the disarmingly naive ones like MCA and BPM, 'maximum credible accident' and (believe it or not) 'best possible means' – though I have lain awake pondering MCAs: credible to whom? In the solemn words of one report, 'There has been a fundamental difficulty in defining Maximum Credible Accident . . . as there is no framework of experience to establish the maximum that is credible.' Yet as the Report of the Royal Commission on Environmental Pollution under Sir Brian Flowers rather optimistically said in 1976, 'It is important that the discussion should be well-informed and as far as possible dispassionate' – which cannot mean disinterested or uncommitted. Both this and the World Council of Churches' Report, *Facing up to Nuclear Power*, are models of fair and balanced presentations, as is the everyman's guide, *Nuclear Choice*, just published by the Church of England's Board of Social Responsibility. There has also been the important conference in 1979 of the World Council of Churches on Faith, Science and the Future, section VI of which was concerned with Energy for the Future.

It is highly desirable if possible to keep a cool head. For those who idolize and those who demonize nuclear power simply play into each others' hands. *Per se* atomic power is neutral, and indeed the National Council of Churches of the USA began in 1960 by characterizing it as a 'gift from God'. By 1976 in contrast it had passed a resolution calling for a moratorium on the processing and use of plutonium as an energy source and the building of a prototype breeder reactor. In 1979 the WCC conference went further in recommending a five-year moratorium on the construction of *all* new nuclear power plants. For in the interval the pressures on both sides have built up alarmingly. There is not only the greatly increased awareness of the coming energy crisis, compounded by the precariousness and price of even our existing oil-supplies. There is the far more widespread knowledge of the hazards of what were welcomed as 'atoms for peace'. *From Hiroshima to Harrisburg*, to use the title of a book by a pupil of mine, James Garrison, defines an era on which it has become impossible to go back. It is also that we stand now on the threshold of the second nuclear industrial revolution, at the critical transition from 'burners' to 'breeders'. The first generation of nuclear reactors has been using uranium in a very wasteful and inefficient way (as well as producing remarkably little electricity – less than 2% of Britain's total useful energy), and already the end is in sight of cheaply recoverable natural fuel. At projected rates of expansion uranium will not see us much beyond petrol and the end of the century. By then, *if* nothing is done and *if* we go on at the present pace (two enormous if's), there will be an energy-gap of colossal proportions, compared with which any recent bumps in petrol prices will look like pimples. And the race will be to the fortunate and to the strong in a world where already the United States and Canada use the equivalent of 11,500 kilograms of coal per person *per annum* (with Kuwait quickly catching up), compared with 4000 in Western Europe and 32 in Bangladesh.

Into this looming vacuum has been thrown the offer of what has been called the 'Faustian bargain' of an all but inexhaustible source of energy – at a price. What the price is I shall go on to consider. But the offer is the Fast Breeder Reactor (FBR), to which the closest analogy would seem to be the ginger-beer plant. For once it gets going it begins to breed more fuel, in the form of plutonium, than it uses. So instal one of our plants (so the package promises) and your fuel problems will be solved – for ever. Even if, like Japan for instance or Indiá, you have few natural resources, you can have a self-sufficient, inflation-proof supply of all the energy you will ever need. It is scarcely surprising that the pressures on developing countries to 'go nuclear' – and on the multi-national corporations to sell it to them – have proved almost irresistible. By 1984 it has been estimated that 32 countries will be operating or, more likely with the delays endemic to such programmes, expecting to operate nuclear reactors, and at the United Nations Habitat conference in Vancouver only one of the developing countries (Papua-New Guinea) opposed nuclear energy. At first of course it will be the 'burner' type. Indeed the 'breeder' will not begin to be commercial until well into next century. Yet such is the lead-time for this sort of technology that we must make our decisions now – whether for that *or for other alternatives* – if we are not to be caught short.

Specifically in Britain it is a question – if we are to pursue this path at all (and to that I shall return) – of three options. (1) We build more of our own AGRs (Advanced Gas-Cooled Reactors), which have been relatively safe but dogged with escalating costs and technical troubles. Only two of the five ordered in 1965 have ever fed power into the grid and the remaining three are six, eight and ten years behind schedule! Yet the Government, with the backing of the Opposition, has just placed an order for two more. (2) We import the American PWR (Pressurized Water Reactor) of the 'Harrisburg' type, of which the Report of the President's Commission stated, 'We are convinced that an accident like Three Mile Island was eventually inevitable.' The Government still hopes to proceed with these if and when a modified design (at substantially increased cost) passes a public enquiry. (3) We press ahead with building the CFR1, the first Commercial Fast Reactor, the forerunner, it has been estimated, if we were to meet all our needs from this source, of some 80 round our coasts. Yet, though FBRs are supposed to be able to produce 60 times more energy per tonne of uranium than thermal reactors, (*a*) they require many years' operation of thermal reactors to manufacture enough plutonium to prime the pump. There are probably about five tonnes of this in the UK at present, and, depending on how much is reserved for 'independent deterrent' warheads (proudly to be 'made in Britain'), the existing nuclear programme might make another ten tonnes by the year 2000 – still enough for only *one* FBR; (*b*) the cost is likely to be about five times that of a thermal reactor; and (*c*) it is not yet known whether a safe large FBR can be built, and small ones would produce even more expensive electricity.

This brings us to the price of the whole bargain. There is first, quite literally, the enormous initial (and by all past experience constantly escalating) cost of installation – which in the present economic climate is bound to pre-empt many other options. Indeed it has been estimated that the capital cost of a nuclear power station, if spent instead on conservation, would save three times more energy than the station would produce in its life-time – and this ignores the running costs and those of fuel, transmission lines, reprocessing plant, *and* of what you do to 'decommission' these highly dangerous pieces of plant once their useful life is over.

Next there is the fuel itself, plutonium, a man-made substance with a radioactive half-life of 24,000 years. Some of it has of course already been produced, in non-usable form, and its reprocessing, especially from other more quake-prone parts of the globe, is already a political hot potato. But this is nothing to what we should be faced with in the future. If a millionth of a gramme is enough to produce lung cancer, can one envisage the handling of the 15–20 tonnes required to produce one FBR?

Then there is the continuing risk of operational accident. The record in Britain so far, it must be recognized, is relatively good compared with other countries and other industries and it would be unjust to single out the Atomic Energy Authority as a whipping-boy. Standards and safeguards have, very properly, been a great deal more stringent than those which the chemical disasters at Flixborough and Seveso have shown us prepared hitherto to tolerate elsewhere. Much care and concern have unquestionably been exercised. Yet so have they, with no expense spared, in the space-programme, and things can still go disconcertingly wrong. Unsettling accounts of near-misses and seepage even from current operations keep coming to light. The Harrisburg accident revealed fundamental faults in design, quite apart from a major factor of human error. The recent power-failure at the French reprocessing plant at La Hague near Cherbourg in April 1980, where a serious accident was averted only because no fuel elements happened to be being treated at the time, disclosed that the regular and the emergency electricity supplies were carried by the *same* lines! Significantly the only part of the plant to have independent generators was not the critical cooling system and monitoring computer but the electric fence round the perimeter, which, the main trade union at the plant commented, 'symbolizes the management's preoccupation' with external as opposed to internal safeguards. This was the second serious accident there in two months. In January pipes carrying radioactive waste under the sea burst and had twice to be repaired.

One can only concur with the dictum that 'whatever it is not impossible for people to do incorrectly is inevitable'. The statistics which are beginning to emerge on the deaths and malfunctions, particularly among children, within the radius of Three Mile Island merely compound the evidence, especially from Germany and elsewhere in the United States, of the increased cancers and leukaemias from low-level radiation in the neighbourhood of nuclear installations *even where no accident has taken place at all.* (This is not to mention the hazards from uranium mining, where Navaho Indians and Australian Aborigines have been exposed to conditions which would be totally unacceptable in white areas.) If the accident at Harrisburg had really got out of hand and resulted in a melt-down, as it so nearly did, it is inconceivable that there would not have been an immediate public demand for the shut-down of all such reactors. In other words, any energy programme dependent on nuclear power will constantly be at the mercy of irresistible pressures in a democratic society which are bound to make it an unreliable source of supply, even if all the technical problems were ironed out.

But of course the problems are far from being licked – above all that of disposing of the wastes, some of which are lethal for longer than human history has yet been recorded. As one of the leading scientific advocates of nuclear energy has said, 'The price we demand of society for this energy source is both a vigilance and a longevity of our social institutions that we are quite unaccustomed to.' That is putting it mildly! Even if we could find ways of sinking it safely in vitrified form in stable rock-formations or below the ocean-bed – and it is quite possible that we could, if we are prepared for the economic (and the political) cost – the thought of the transport involved is itself sobering (let alone the potential rocket-failures in shooting it gaily into space). But the know-how is very far from perfected, and if there is one rule of this road it is surely: 'Do not enter this box unless your exit is clear.' 'Energy now, waste later' should be completely unacceptable. The Royal Commission Report said optimistically: 'We are confident that an acceptable solution will be found and we attach great importance to the search; for we are agreed that it would be irresponsible and morally wrong to commit future generations to the consequences of fission power on a massive scale unless it has been demonstrated beyond reasonable doubt that at least one method exists for the safe isolation of these wastes for the indefinite future.' Yet nothing in the four years that have passed since those words were written gives confidence that such a solution is in sight, let alone in operation. Meanwhile the wastes pile up – no less, it has been calculated, than 76 million cubic feet so far of high- and low-level wastes from military and commercial sources in the US alone!

But it is not only human miscalculation and natural hazards that have to be taken into account but the effect of labour-disputes, civil disturbances, acts of sabotage, revolutions and old-fashioned wars *anywhere in the world*. For what a bomb on a nuclear installation – a prime military target – would release into the atmosphere would certainly not be confined to the country concerned. Here above all no man is an island. One of the more disturbing aspects of even the most responsible advocacy of nuclear power, especially in America, is its isolationism. A few years ago I read a whole supplement of the *Christian Science Monitor* devoted to a full, fair and balanced discussion of the subject – yet nowhere would one have guessed that anyone in the world had an energy-gap but the United States or was actively doing anything about it! And in a carefully argued lecture presented to me by a friend on 'The Case for Nuclear Power' given to the National Academy of Engineering in Washington I could not help noticing the blinkers: 'Another concern', said the professor from the Massachussetts Institute of Technology, 'often expressed about nuclear power is that it facilitates the spread of nuclear weapons to countries which do not now have them. This is unfortunately true if such countries build reprocessing plants, but it is not a valid argument against the extended use of nuclear energy within the United States'!

This brings us to the risks of international terrorism. Of course for most of the time the stuff is literally unapproachable, and therefore looks after itself. But if and where it can be leaked, stolen or hi-jacked, especially in the course of transport, then as the Royal Commission itself recognized, we must be certain that it will be. To render the unthinkable thinkable the boffins at this point play their war-games. Suppose, I was being told in America, a terrorist group drove a ship into New York harbour and threatened to blow it up.

Of course we should have to concede whatever they asked for – for you couldn't be sure they weren't bluffing. But what could they demand, ultimately, that we could not give – mostly no doubt (though that wasn't said) at someone else's expense? Yet where does *that* Danegeld lead?

But suppose, as we are assured, you *could* concentrate it all in anaesthetized nuclear 'parks' with their own priesthood and bodyguard, above military coup (how?) or industrial sabotage, the internal security required to prevent its diversion or even the unauthorized dissemination of knowledge could be used to justify almost any restriction of civil liberties. Here again are the measured words of the Royal Commission: 'What is most to be feared is an insidious growth in surveillance . . . to a degree that would be regarded as wholly unacceptable but which could not then be avoided because of the extent of our dependence on plutonium for energy supplies.' The UK Atomic Energy Authority already has its own police force, the only private one in the country. Its members are empowered to carry firearms, including machine-guns, and to engage in 'hot pursuit' of any suspect; and their activities are cloaked by the Official Secrets Act. For the theft of plutonium by a terrorist group or its leaking to another country (in the piratical manner in which Israel originally acquired its uranium) is indeed a veritable nightmare. A few pounds of the stuff would be enough to make a perfectly workable atomic bomb – or threaten contamination for countless generations. One has merely to envisage it in the hands of the IRA or the PLO, or some Amin or Gadafi, or even of such legitimate states as Israel or South Africa or Brazil, none of which has signed the nuclear non-proliferation treaty. For ultimately *no one* believes that atoms for peace, exported for rich profit, cannot be turned into atoms for war. Indeed it has been questioned whether there have been any overseas sales of nuclear plant where the objective was solely to produce energy and not weapons. Iran, for instance, was building four reactors when the revolution fortunately created such a severe balance of payments crisis that they had to be stopped. Iraq is also building. But *why* should these oil-rich countries wish to import an incompletely developed technique to produce energy at 5–10 times the cost of their own supplies?

So what conclusion is to be drawn? I began by thinking, with the Royal Commission, that a completely non-nuclear future was unrealistic even as a goal, let alone as a probable prospect. But I am more and more inclined to the view that the nuclear option is an expensive and dangerous irrelevance. The Fast Breeder is in any case of no immediate relevance to bridging the gap left by the drying up of oil. Even the present thermal reactors if pressed on with to the maximum of the Government's (modified) programme would only provide some 5% of the electricity we now get from oil and gas – or 3½% of our total useful energy. *Except* therefore for creating plutonium for missile warheads, they too are but marginally relevant to the critical period (c. 2000–2025) when oil will be reduced to the dribble that will have to be reserved for chemical feedstock. In other words, we have basically to solve this problem by other means – and having done so there seems no point in reverting thereafter to such a highly dangerous and uncertain form of energy production. For by then there can be no return to huge industrial growth-rates, since many of the vital metals so wastefully used in our century will also be disappearing.

What then is the alternative if the nuclear option is set on one side?

The layman is at the mercy of projections and scenarios that are bewilderingly various and disconcertingly subject to revision. Yet a sustainable nuclear-free society is apparently by no means the mirage which it has so often been painted. In the course of 1979 two publications appeared which seriously questioned earlier presuppositions. The first is by Gerald Leach and members of the International Institute for Environment and Development, *A Low Energy Strategy for the United Kingdom*. It seeks to demonstrate 'systematically, and in detail, how the UK could have fifty years of prosperous material growth and yet use less primary energy than it does today'. The second, from the Energy Project at Harvard Business School, *Energy Future* (ed. R. Stobaugh and D. Yergin), similarly claims that the USA could use 30–40% less energy than it does 'with virtually no penalty for the way Americans live'. These are hard-headed and sober estimates of what can be saved by using established techniques of increased efficiency from present energy sources. Again Sir Martin Ryle, the Nobel prize-winner and Astronomer Royal, to whom I am greatly indebted for suggestions, comments and corrections, has recently put out from the Cavendish Laboratory at Cambridge a document, 'The UK Energy Problem', earlier summarized in *The Observer*, and now published in the magazine *Resurgence* (May-June 1980), which similarly argues that by systematic methods of conservation and much greater funding into the exploration and exploitation of renewable energy, from the sun, wind, waves, the earth and organic sources, there is absolutely no need to go nuclear.

Leach with his co-workers concludes that 'nuclear power in our projections becomes almost a side issue' and 'the fast breeder reactor and associated reprocessing and traffic in plutonium . . . a costly and dangerous irrelevance'. He even questions whether it is really necessary to develop new sources of electricity from wind and wave. But Ryle doubts this and cites figures to show that in the US the President's Council on Environmental Quality concluded that at least 25% of present delivered energy could by the year 2000 be provided by renewable sources (mostly wind and small-scale hydro). A figure of 44% is quoted for Denmark by 2000 and for Canada of 100% by 2025. Yet the UK Department of Energy continues to state that the figure for Britain can only be 5% by the end of the century. As Ryle says, 'This may well be true so long as virtually all research and development funding is directed to nuclear programmes. In the case of wind – the most promising for the UK – the *total* R and D funds over the past 25 years have been £0.97 million (about one *day's* subsidy to British Leyland).'

What they all agree on is that by conservation we can, and must, curb our profligate consumption of irreplaceable resources without any serious loss of energy. Figures again for layman are difficult to check, but impressive savings are seemingly available simply by more efficient equipment and insulation. Thus Ryle quotes a Danish analysis showing that a household spending an additional $146 on domestic equipment using better electric motors, drives and insulation on refrigerators and ovens, etc, could save $1,588 of generating capacity! In Britain a recent official report from the Transport and Road Research Laboratory estimates that better design could save 60% of car fuel – incidentally well beyond Leach's figure of 40–50%. If the Government were prepared, say, to give 95% grants for approved schemes for loft insulation, instead of the derisory sum at present offered (unbelievably just *cut* from £50 to £25 and abolished altogether for council houses!), it could get immensely better value for money than by sinking it in nuclear power-stations – or by leaving fuel to ration itself by price, with all its inflationary and socially divisive consequences. The great advantage, socially speaking, of all such conservationist and 'soft' energy-programmes, apart from the sheer saving to hard-pressed individuals' pockets, is that they are labour-intensive and would provide employment in areas where it is most needed.

In Britain above all, we have a greater opportunity than many countries to try to show the world a more excellent way. For we have more generating capacity for electricity at present than we can use and we have coal and for the time being oil. We need not be stampeded, despite pressures from the hawks of atomic energy. Yet a *mere* moratorium only delays and deepens the crisis – driving others to replace with nuclear energy the fossil fuels we are meanwhile consuming. The counter-argument that if the rich nations do not go nuclear we shall be depriving the third world of the oil and coal which alone it will be able to afford is highly suspect. The only policy that will preserve the fossil fuels *for anyone* is a drastic programme, led by the energy guzzlers, to cut waste and switch to renewable sources, and in the meantime to use, and where necessary import, more coal and natural gas. What oil there is will undoubtedly go to the highest bidder, and nuclear power will in any case be able in the short- and middle-term future to save precious little of it.

Can we use the respite afforded by our relatively fortunate position to discover what a 'just, participatory and sustainable society' (to use the WCC's formula) means which does not depend on a highly centralized and vulnerable technology – such as in due course a fusion-powered society (though relatively beneficent compared with fission) would also be? Are we yet mature enough to demonstrate that there are some things we can do but won't, that creativity in science as in art comes from restraint, that power is declared most chiefly in showing mercy and pity, that the fear of the Lord is the beginning of wisdom? Only by our example can we hope to persuade developing countries that the plutonium path may *not* be the way to true independence and self-sufficiency.

Ultimately we must face the question, and face it now, of what kind of a Britain, what kind of a world, do we want? Let me end, not with a predigested answer to that question, but with three quotations to ponder. The first is from Aldous Huxley, who said as long ago as 1946: 'All countries embarking on a nuclear power programme will have to be totalitarian.' The second is from a Bangalore physicist, quoted in a lecture I heard by John Habgood, formerly a Research Fellow in physics at King's College, Cambridge, and now Bishop of Durham: 'Technology is like genetic material: it carries with it the code of that society.' For nuclear energy implies a certain sort of society for its own maintenance: its introduction is as portentous, and as irreversible, as that of the plough. The third is a gnomic utterance of a twentieth-century prophet, Eugene Rosenstock-Huessy, with whom I once had the privilege of staying: 'Every new invention expands space, shortens time and destroys community.'

Yet sensing themselves under a similar pressure of the shortening of time the early Christians did not despair or live to themselves. They set out to redeem the time. To what looked to them like the end of the world they reacted with the writer of II Peter: 'Think what sort of people you ought to be, what devout and dedicated lives you should live!' For through and out the other side of something greater even than the Maximum Credible Accident they said, 'We have his promise, and look forward to new heavens and a new earth, the home of justice' (II Peter 3.11–13). Nuclear power choices are *not* for the Christian the ultimate ones. Yet for our generation, they may be the penultimate. And this is where Bonhoeffer insisted the Christian ethic has to be lived and worked out: in the name of the ultimate to take with radical seriousness the things before the last.

IX

SOME LEAVES OF THE TREE

1. ZACCHAEUS

He was a little man, he was very rich, he was a superintendent of taxes, he was a climber, he was a Jew. Not a formula for instant social acceptability. 'Even for a just man', said St Paul, 'one of us would hardly die, though perhaps for a good man one might actually brave death; but Christ died for us while we were yet sinners' – and this man was *ex officio* a sinner in the eyes of his contemporaries. Accepting the unacceptable – that is the heart and glory of the Christian gospel. Yet instinctively we think of it applying to the unacceptable in others – like that unattractive swot or creep or wog – and we feel: 'How marvellous, Christ has accepted him – glad I've not got to.' But salvation is in the first place about accepting the unacceptable in ourselves – and not only *Christ* accepting it, so that we can now off-load it on to him instead of projecting it on to others. It is about *us* being enabled to accept the unacceptable in ourselves, so that we can be made *whole.* And that is a good deal harder and takes a good deal longer – so that the New Testament talks about those who are *being* saved. Not even Christ offers instant salvation, though the process may *start*, as in St Paul's case, in a sudden confrontation with the person we really are.

So let us use the pen-portrait of Zacchaeus (Luke 19.1–10) as a picture of ourselves, and those unclubbable traits of his as delineaments of what Jung called the shadow in each one of us – that side of us which is not in itself sinful but which we would rather not have to acknowledge or live with, the things about us which we repress or work off on other people. What the marks of that shadow are will of course differ with each one of us. But try a few of Zacchaeus's for a fit.

He was a little man. Haven't most of us got that little man inside us, suffering secretly from a deep sense of inferiority, longing to be recognized and accepted – and yet inwardly fearing to be? He's always at the back of the crowd, jostled, or swamped by numbers. He'd do anything, he thinks, to get on top – just for a few more inches there, or that man's ease, or this man's graces. But if Zacchaeus had thought beforehand that Jesus would actually stop the crowd and point up at him, I bet he'd never have had the courage to do it. As I overheard a girl saying in the street the other day, he was 'caught between the embarrassment of being noticed and the fear of not being noticed at all'.

Secondly, he was very rich. As William Davis the former editor of *Punch* has said in the title of his book on economics, *It's no Sin to be Rich*. Yet we're shamefaced about wealth, about privilege, about schooling, and even in a university we deprecate academic excellence. There's a WASP (a White Anglo-Saxon Protestant) trying in each one of us (if we *are* one) to 'keep a low profile' (and if we aren't to conceal the chip). And if we really *are* very rich, in anything, we'd prefer people didn't know it.

Then he was a superintendent of taxes. Who would admit even to himself that that's what he really wanted to be? Yet we all have our secret ambitions, our fantasies of 'arriving' some day. There is the top man, the tycoon, the successful television personality, waiting to get out (even of the ineffectual don). And we covertly envy or resent those who have made it.

He was a climber. This of course takes endlessly subtle forms. I once had a tutor who literally on a walk would sheer up a tree. Cambridge is no place for a mountaineer manqué. But there's the eager beaver in all of us. We are a mass of suppressed desires, and some of them entirely good: like Zacchaeus, we would really rather like to see what Jesus looked like – but we would never dare let on.

Then he too was 'a son of Abraham'. That was a pretty well buried fact about him till Jesus drew it out. Some of us are quite deeply religious – yet we can't admit it to ourselves or to the society we keep. Dag Hammarskjøld was one of those. He kept a spiritual diary, called *Markings*, found at his death – yet the mores of secular Sweden would never let him acknowledge the fact even to his family.

Sin, or alienation, has to do with the fact that we can't accept ourselves – or large parts of ourselves. Justification by faith is, as Tillich put it, accepting the fact that we are accepted – the whole of us. And that is extraordinarily hard to believe or to live with. 'Salvation' for the Bible is so much bigger a word than the biblicists have made it. It is what St Peter called 'this perfect wholeness', integration both individual and social. The Son of Man, the proper man, comes to seek and to save what is lost, oppressed or suppressed – and he does it by saying to us, 'I must come and stay with you today.' And the test of salvation is freedom, feasting, giving away, letting go. It isn't all champagne corks popping. The final criterion, as St Paul says, of whether God's love has flooded our inmost hearts – right down to the core – is whether we can 'endure' and exult even in our sufferings, turning even the unacceptable into material of praise. Such is the life of the man or woman who is being made whole, on the way to that mature manhood which is measured by nothing less than the full stature of Christ.

But what is this 'stature' of Christ? It is the same word used to say that Zacchaeus was small in stature. And the real question is whether our Christ, made in our image, may not be too small to save. The Christ 'invited in' in much evangelism and piety can actually have a narrowing effect. Jung has rightly I think accused Christians of weakening the Christ-image by splitting off the shadow side, which, again, is not in itself evil, and projecting it on to an irreconcilable counterpart, the Antichrist. The effect of this is to make Christ less than completely human. For only a person who has not cut off part of himself can be free to relate to men and women as Jesus did. To accept the unacceptable in others depends on not finding it a threat to oneself. Jesus is the one who 'became man', not, as much Christian theology has depicted it, by becoming a man from having been something else (no one, not even God, can do that, though as a genuine product of the evolutionary process he can also be God's timeless Word to it), but, uniquely, by *becoming* fully and totally human. As the writer to the Hebrews boldly puts it, he was 'made perfect', which does not mean that he morally improved but that he achieved integration in the only way men can grow, by acceptance and incorporation of the whole self rather than by rejection and repression of a part. And, the writer makes it clear, this was no automatic or effortless superiority: it was wrought out of blood and sweat and tears. The struggle to accept the unacceptable comes through most vividly, as I suggested earlier, in the vignette of Jesus in the gospels dealing with the Canaanite woman (Matt. 15.21–8). He began, evidently, with all the inbuilt racial prejudices, repressions and alienations which made up a genuine Palestinian Jew of the first century. The miracle is not that he didn't start with them but that he transcended and transformed them: he learnt from the things he suffered, he emerged a different and a bigger man.

L. W. Grensted the psychologist suggestively drew attention to the way in Jesus' life-struggle in which the unacceptable is presented in the gospels as progressively internalized and absorbed. In the wilderness temptations it is objectivized and projected on to the devil. At the Transfiguration the cross is represented 'not by Satan, but by the friendly figures of Moses and Elijah'. In Gethsemane there is 'no longer . . . a casting out of those elements in humanity which are the source of the conflict', but in a final shuddering struggle, which St Mark introduces with the words 'he began to be panic-stricken and distraught', the embracing of them as the will of the Father. 'He had to be made like his brethren in every respect', says the writer to the Hebrews again, 'so that he might *become* a merciful and faithful high priest' (2.17). For only so could he save or salve others, only so could he communicate to them *his* 'peace', his wholeness.

But, finally, if Christ is according to the classical formula 'complete (*teleios*) in regard to his manhood', so also, if he is to save, must he be *totus deus*, through and through what God is. But if so then we must be prepared to have our image of God stretched in the same way. For, as Jung also saw, especially in his *Answer to Job*, Christians have done to God what they have done to Christ. They have identified him with a goodness which excludes rather than incorporates evil. Charles Davis has elaborated this in his book *Body as Spirit*, in a notable chapter on 'the inhumanity of evil'. Christianity's unique emphasis on the devil represents God's unconsciously produced shadow: the mystery of iniquity is placed alongside the mystery of goodness and cast out of heaven. But 'if', he says, 'we take the polarity of good and evil as we find them in human existence, and then identify God the Absolute with a goodness excluding evil, we make it impossible for us to accept ourselves radically. . . . The devil represents all that we will not acknowledge in ourselves. . . . When . . . evil is disowned it becomes terrifyingly inhuman.' And God himself 'formed in the image of a self-righteous monarch, cut off from all the pain and suffering, the frailty and the sin of this world, personified moral goodness made absolute' becomes a very devil, Blake's Nobodaddy, rather than the God and Father of our Lord Jesus Christ.

To reach the God of love we must go back to the God who is the ground of *all* being, of the impersonal and the evil as well as the moral, of volcanoes and tapeworms and cancer as much as of everything else. And this is the God of the Old Testament. 'I form light and create darkness, I make weal and create woe, I am the Lord, who do all these things' (Isa. 45.7) – or in another passage from the same prophet in the blunt version of the Good News Bible: 'I create the blacksmith, who builds a fire and forges weapons. I also create the soldier who uses the weapons to kill' (Isa. 54.16). Yes, God has many faces and many hands, like the Hindu god Shiva whose energies stream forth in the dance of life, terrifying and benevolent. If as Christians we dare to say that in the human face of God, in Christ and him crucified, we see the clue to the rest, it is only because it accepts and transforms all the rest – 'at the last through wood and nails'. God is *not* evil, in the only sense which Kant saw was ultimately evil, that of the evil will. He is love; but a love which all along is taking up, changing, Christifying everything.

The God of Zacchaeus, the Father of the Son of Man, is the God who seeks rather than rejects, who saves rather than negates, the lost, the oppressed and the repressed, who is no more outside evil than anything else. As the writer to the Hebrews says once again, 'We do not yet see all things subjected', integrated, perfected, 'but we see Jesus' (2.8f.). In the mass of nature and history, both without and within ourselves, the reduction of all to the purposes of spirit, the vanquishing of 'vanity' by love, seems utterly remote and obscure. Over most of the processes of what Teilhard de Chardin called this 'personalizing' universe it is still waste and void and darkness. But for the Christian a light has shone in the darkness, in the face of Jesus Christ, which the darkness cannot quench. And out of that darkness and into the shadow of our most unacceptable selves comes the word that Zacchaeus heard: 'Be quick and come down; *I* must come and stay with you today.'

2. THE UNJUST STEWARD

If the parable of the workers in the vineyard (Matt. 20.1–16), with its equal pay for grossly unequal work, would be anathema to the Trades Union Congress, that of the unjust steward (Luke 16.1–13), with its sanctioning of the unacceptable face of capitalism, would cause splutterings in the Confederation of British Industry – on the assumption, that is, that either was being recommended by the gospels as a wages policy or a code of management practice. In the first the employer is generous with his own money – 'Have I not the right to do what I like with my own?' In the second the bailiff is being generous with someone else's money – fiddling the accounts at the firm's expense. Yet both are commended!

This second parable indeed is such a corker that from the very beginning the church has not known quite what to do with it. It was evidently a problem in the Sunday school at Caesarea, or wherever St Luke's gospel was written; for at the end of the story no less than five morals are appended – introduced by the phrase 'So I say to you'. It is quite possible that they are separate sayings of Jesus himself, but as interpretations of the parable they are clearly the work of those attempting to render it acceptable. Two are apparently contradictory ('Use your worldly wealth to win friends' and 'You cannot serve God and money') and three unexceptionable moral generalizations: 'The man who can (or cannot) be trusted in little things can (or cannot) be trusted in big things', 'If you have not proved trustworthy with this world's wealth, who will trust you with the wealth that is real?', and 'If you have proved untrustworthy with what belongs to another, who will give you what is your own?'. They are all ways of trying to make the story inoffensive – and it can't be done. For its point lies in the punchline: 'The master applauded the dishonest bailiff for acting so astutely.' And whether 'the master' is the employer or Jesus makes little difference. What should apparently be condemned is being condoned.

It is more than likely that the story is of an actual event that was going the rounds at the time. 'Have you heard what happened the other day up on Lord X's estate?' Perhaps people had told it to Jesus, expecting him to condemn the shady dealings – like the prophets before him. Perhaps he told it to them, but with a twist in the tail.

Anyway this character was accused of being up to no good. 'What's this I hear?', says the landlord, 'You're fired. Turn in your accounts' – not, evidently, for inspection to see whether he had been dishonest (that is assumed) but to determine, before he quits, how much he owes. There is no suggestion that he could not have got the full amount from his master's creditors. But he has his eye on the future. What's he going to do for a living when he is thrown out? He couldn't stand a manual job and he couldn't face his friends on assistance. 'I've got it', he says, 'I'll put them all in *my* debt – and it won't cost me a penny!' So he calls in the creditors one by one, not simply the two instanced, but each of them, singly, so that none of the others would realize what was going on. This is how such things are always worked, and when the enquiry is set up into the slush fund it is surprising how no one seems to know. For here we are dealing with the big fish, not the minnows. The merchants involved were evidently wholesalers and the sums considerable. The discounts given appear to be curiously different (what's he up to?, we think) – one gets 50% off, the other only 20%. But he has calculated it pretty precisely, since the value of olive-oil and wheat was different. In each case the rake-off would have worked out much the same, about 500 denarii – 500 times the sum involved in the vineyard wages dispute! That's the sort of sweetener which middle management is talking about. So the final comment, the 'shock headline' of the modern newspaper report, is all the more stunning: 'The master applauded the dishonest bailiff for acting so astutely. For the worldly', he said, 'are more astute than the other-worldly in dealing with their own kind.'

But observe what is being commended. It's not the man's shady practice but his shrewdness. In his fix he thought quickly and thought cleverly – though evidently not quite cleverly enough: for the truth came out. The worldly are more astute in dealing with their 'own kind', or, as the old version has it, 'generation'. In the short term they get away with it – whatever may finally come out in the wash. But at least they deal with the present. Their action is not too late – nor, as we have seen, too little. They know how to respond to a crisis – unlike 'the sons of light' (the very phrase we now know the Dead Sea covenanters, and no doubt other good churchmen, used of themselves – rather like 'the Festival of Light' in our day). For, faced with the challenge of Jesus and the claims of the kingdom, what did *they* do? Precisely too little and too late. 'Can't you *see*?', Jesus is saying to his religious contemporaries. 'Let this man teach you a thing or two.'

So what is the message of the parable? Try to moralize it, as most preachers do to most parables, and you find yourself in a mess. You make God immoral, a spokesman for injustice. But Jesus seems to have had no compunction about representing the central figure of his stories as less than reputable. The creditor of one parable puts the unforgiving debtor to the torturers. The crusty old judge of another won't see the widow given her rights till he is badgered to exasperation. Equally if you try to give the story a pious ending you finish up with the kind of platitudes with which from the start the church has sought to make it safe.

What therefore is the lesson we should draw? Perhaps it is to be found in the question with which Jesus started another parable (for he was always putting questions rather than giving take-away answers): 'Who then is the faithful and wise steward?' (Luke 12.42). For this is the very combination of qualities lacking in the central character of our story. He was shrewd, but unfaithful; and there are plenty of his type in the world. It's easy too to be faithful, but clueless; and we see many of them about – not least in the churches. But what Jesus requires of his followers is to be as 'wise as serpents' *and* as 'harmless as doves' (Matt. 10.16). Moreover he calls them to be 'stewards'. Now stewards are middle-men – like the centurion in the gospel story with men over him and men under him. They operate in what these days would be called the 'service' area of the economy. And, whatever his particular slot in society, this is the model of the Christian's life: he is responsible to, and responsible for. And in this he has to be both 'faithful' and 'wise' – in that order.

First, he is to be a person of utter integrity wherever he is set, in big things or in small, in dealing with his own or with another's, with material wealth or with the values of the spirit (and perhaps we can see how the secondary applications may all come back). He puts the unconditional first and, come what may, can be trusted to do so. There is simply no substitute for that sort of fidelity – and nothing may be drawn from our parable to qualify or question it.

But then he is also to be wise – and that not simply in dealing with his own kind but to God. He's got to be up to what *he's* up to, reading the signs of the times, spiritually alert and politically astute. For the moral and spiritual issues are usually concealed in the technical and material, and the points of faithfulness are constantly shifting and shading off into others. That is why the worldly are commended for being wise 'in their own generation', at the point and place of decision. The Christian too in his position of answerability both to God and neighbour is equally reminded that the Son of Man comes looking for faith in 'this generation' – not just timelessly nor merely at some terminal moment of history, but in the decisiveness of each recurring hour of salvation and day of judgment.

> Once to every man and nation
> Comes the moment to decide,. . .
> And the choice goes by for ever
> 'Twixt that darkness and that light.

The 'unjust steward' has got a bad name – quite literally. For the traditional names of the parables (where did they come from?), like headlines, are often misleading. Thus 'the prodigal son' is the climax of a series in Luke 15, of 'the lost sheep' and 'the lost coin', and should undoubtedly be called 'the lost son'. Equally, 'the wicked husbandmen' sets the emphasis in the wrong place. It is followed by the saying about 'the stone which the builders rejected', and they are perhaps linked by an underlying pun on the Hebrew *ben*, son, and *eben*, stone. In any case it would be better called 'the rejected son'. So here it is not the unjustness of the steward which is fastened on for comment but his shrewdness. The Scots might call it the parable of 'the canny bailiff'. In fact it is never actually said that he was a twister in the first place. He was accused, and the word used suggests slanderously or maliciously, of 'wasting' the property – the same term used of the prodigal son in squandering his substance. In other words his crime, unproven, was prodigality, wasteful management, and his sacking, before the accounts were even opened, would undoubtedly today qualify as 'wrongful dismissal'. It was afterwards that he was shown to be the wheeler-dealer which doubtless he was.

Nevertheless 'the canny bailiff' is an unexpected leaf on the tree of life. He is definitely deciduous. Yet he catches the light and serves as a foil. Jesus invites us to stop for a while, look up, take a lesson – and then, in part, to go and do likewise.

3. JUDAS

When I announced that I was to preach on Judas in a course in Trinity Chapel on Bible Characters Re-assessed, one of our Fellows said, 'Are you going to do for Judas what I did for Ethelred the Unready?' If by that is meant rehabilitate him, as people now rehabilitate Richard III or even Richard Nixon, the answer is, No. Yet he is certainly material for re-assessment. For he raises a host of unanswered – and ultimately unanswerable – questions.

Jesus's judgment on him was that it would have been better for him if he had never been born (Mark 14.21). But in that case why did he choose him – and after a night spent in prayer? What did he see in him – and what went wrong? The more we black Judas, as the early church not unnaturally did, the more by implication we question Jesus as a judge of character. We cannot avoid the conclusion that Judas was one of his failures. But when and how and why did the worm get into him? St John says that Jesus knew from the beginning who would betray him, but he says the same also of those who did not believe in him, and this like so much else in this gospel is to be read as retrospective theological interpretation, not as psychological insight into Jesus's consciousness at the time. Certainly it is not meant in any sense which removes responsibility or free will. It is comparable rather with the insight of the poem 'Germinal' (by 'A.E.'), quoted by Graham Greene, that 'In the lost boyhood of Judas Christ was betrayed'. There were factors, as we should put it, that went right back.

Of course, like most else, this is speculation. Yet the very name 'Iscariot' may contain a clue. Some have derived it from *sicarius*, the dagger man, a term Josephus uses of the Jewish freedom-fighters. But much more likely, since it is also the name of his father Simon (John 6.71), it indicates, as some manuscripts interpret it, *ish Kerioth*, the man of Kerioth in the Negeb, down in the deep south. The rest of the twelve, as far as we know, were Galileans (cf. Acts 1.11; 2.7). With the tensions between Judaea and Galilee and the disdain of southerners for the north, that could have made him a loner. To become treasurer of the group he must have had a head on his shoulders, as his quick calculation shows of the waste involved in that extremely expensive perfume poured on Jesus – 300 denarii, the best part of a year's wages for a working man, for just 12 ounces (John 12.3–5). Compared with that the price of betrayal, 30 shekels, was pretty trivial – which makes it the more unlikely that he did it just for the money, even if, as St John suggests, he was not above petty pilfering (12.6). Indeed it is only Matthew who represents him as asking for money (26.15). In the other synoptists it seems almost to be pressed upon him – and John does not even mention it. But this is all part of the confused evidence about his end. According to Matthew (27.3–10), in a fit of remorse Judas flung down the money in the temple, went off and hanged himself; and the chief priests, because it was the price of blood, decided they couldn't devote it to sacred use but put it to buying a cemetery for foreigners. Acts (1.18f.) has an entirely different story: Judas himself bought the field, without returning the money, fell headlong in it, and it was called Bloody Acre because his guts poured out. Reconciling that is a challenge to the fundamentalist, because he can't have died twice – and there's yet a third tradition quoted by the Fathers, which seems to have established itself independently of scripture, that he swelled to a gross size and was squelched by a cart! Obviously no end was too bad for him.

But *why* did he betray Jesus? Again, we shall never know. But that hasn't prevented poets and novelists trying their hand. One of the more careful was Dorothy Sayers in her cycle of broadcast plays

The Man Born to be King, who approached it with the mind of a detective writer. Her character-analysis was, as you would expect, subtle and still reads well. She thought Judas became convinced that Jesus was going to betray his own cause by selling out to the Zealots. To forestall this he led the authorities to arrest him – as they did – as a revolutionary (Mark 14.48). When he discovered that he had misread Jesus he was filled with remorse. But this, like other reconstructions to save Jesus from himself, makes Judas a bit too single-mindedly spiritual to be credible. Most interpreters put the boot on the other foot – and I should agree with them.

The first time that the unreliability of Judas is mentioned in the gospels is after the desert-feeding in St John – when there is a surge to make Jesus king and march on Jerusalem (6.15). Evidently Jesus cannot trust the twelve not to go along with this hope; for according to Mark's account he 'compels' them to get in a boat, packs them off across the lake, and only then disperses the crowd (6.45). Later he has to test the terms of the disciples' loyalty. Led by Peter they affirm it, but have forcibly to be detached from their image of him as a triumphalist Messiah in favour of that of the suffering Son of Man (Mark 8.27–33). In fact in Mark Jesus uses much the same language of Peter as in John he uses of Judas – both are described as 'Satan'. Peter, as we know, came round to the need for suffering and death – though not without *his* betrayal of the Master and his final show of violence in Gethsemane. Could Jesus see even then that Judas was not convinced? 'Have I not chosen you, all twelve? Yet one of you is a devil' (John 6.70). And when later he cooled yet another demo (St John's account of the triumphal entry (12.12–15) makes it, I think more probably, a defusing of a popular ovation rather than a planned procession), was this for Judas the last straw? For it is after this, on top of that criminal waste of good money, that he decides to act. Jesus must be made to show his hand and seize his chance of power. If he wouldn't, then he, Judas, would provoke the confrontation which, with all that was going for him at the time, Jesus must surely win. Passover and the present wave of popular support was an opportunity that could not be allowed to go by. So he slips the information leading to his arrest for which the Sanhedrin had asked (John 11.57), and for which they had doubtless promised a reward. But, we read, 'When he saw that Jesus was *condemned*' – not, observe, when he saw that he, Judas, was mistaken – he realizes that it has misfired calamitously and he tries to 'go back on' it (the word implies no more). But it was too late; and he withdraws defeated and embittered (Matt. 27.3–5).

Now, whether this reconstruction is true to Judas, it is surely highly significant that Matthew and his church still thought, after the event, that Judas's intention was that Jesus should *not* be condemned. Moreover one of the things one has got to explain is why right up to the last moment the rest of the twelve were at a complete loss to know whom Jesus might be referring to at supper, or when Judas got up and left why he did so, or even, apparently, when he showed up in the garden what he had come for. As Dorothy Sayers makes Philip say, reassuringly at that point, 'It's all right – it's all right – it's Judas!' This does not read like the action of a man they had long had reason to suspect. It looks as if he fully went along with them, willing Jesus to win perhaps even more intensely than the others. In fact at the Last Supper much the same is once again said to Peter as to Judas: both would defect. Yet none protested his loyalty more loudly than Peter. Indeed the most poignant moment is when 'one by one', in Mark's vivid phrase (14.19), they all ask, 'Surely it's not I?' No one dared to rule himself out.

And this is where all the speculation and detection, however fascinating, must come to rest. Is it I? For Judas is not only within the twelve – 'one of you who is eating with me' (Mark 14.18,20): that is the depth of the tragedy – but within ourselves. He is the shadow-figure, as Leonardo depicted him, who is a part of each one of us. And it is no good just disowning the shadow or blackening it still further. Observe that Jesus makes no attempt to suppress or restrain Judas. Indeed he goes out of his way to offer him the sop from the common dish. He even tells him to get on with it (John 13.26f). Nor does he throw him out. Judas leaves of his own accord – and the light and the darkness are polarized (John 13.30). But he comes back – out of the dark – with a sign of affection, and still Jesus greets him as 'Friend' (Matt. 26.50f).

The beloved enemy. Of all that I have tried to read round this theme nothing gets it better, I think, than a poignant piece of autobiographical writing by Una Kroll, *Lament for a Lost Enemy*. It is the story of a love-hate relationship which finishes in the other's vindictive suicide. And she ends by reflecting on which of the two was Judas. On the face of it, the one who committed suicide. But had he, or had either of them, loved Jesus deeply enough to betray him? For, as in the moving representation in *Jesus Christ Superstar*, Judas loves Jesus intensely – just as Mary Magdalene loves Jesus – and Jesus loves Judas. Without that dimension there is no tragedy. Yet Judas fails Jesus. *And Jesus fails Judas*. He cannot finally save him from himself. Nor could he save Peter from his denial or spare his mother her suffering or rescue the terrorists who hung beside him or soften the taunting crowds. 'In the cross', she says, 'are to be found all the failures of men and women. And Christ took all these failures and made them his own. He shared our failure.' His death was a real death, and his despair a real despair. In the mysterious providence of God failure is a necessary part of 'the material out of which our wholeness comes' – and 'it will continue until the work of God is finally accomplished'. 'Jesus remains on the cross', said Origen, 'so long as one sinner remains in hell'; and he dared to believe in the redemption of Judas and of the devil. For if Judas is in ourselves, how else *can* we be made whole – if the shadow be not integrated?

4. JULIAN OF NORWICH

Julian of Norwich is someone of whom we know extraordinarily little with any certainty. She is sometimes called Lady Julian, but there is no evidence she was in any way aristocratic, and sometimes Mother Julian, but she ruled no monastic house nor even probably belonged to a religious order. In fact her very name is unknown, 'Julian' being the dedication of the church in Norwich where she had her cell and which has now been beautifully restored. She was an anchoress, an enclosed solitary, and the *Revelations of Divine Love*, which is all she has left behind her, came to her when she was aged thirty, on 8 May 1373, fifteen of them between four and nine in the morning and a concluding one the following night, though it was a long time, she tells us, before the meaning of some of them became clear to her.

She is best known for her oft-quoted assurance that 'All shall be well, and all shall be well, and all manner of thing shall be well.' But this is no facile or complacent optimism, like the motto (believe it or not) of the old Borough of Camberwell, 'All's well'! It derives from an overpowering sense of the love and goodness of God at work in and through everything. In a final reflection on her experiences she said this:

> Love was his meaning. Who showed it to you? Love. What did he show you? Love. Why did he show it? For love. Hold on to this and you will know and understand love more and more. But you will not know or learn anything else – ever!

Hers is above all a theology which starts from the sun and not from the clouds. This doesn't mean that she does not have an acute sense of sin and to us an almost morbid preoccupation with her own supposed sickness to death and Christ's physical sufferings. But the shadow is deep only because the light is so bright. Sin, she says, is 'behovable', that is, it is behoved, necessary, that there shall be sin. And the marring it has introduced is deeply tragic. Yet it is almost a *felix culpa*, a 'happy fault'. For without it we should never have known what love was capable of. 'We see deeds done', she says, 'that are so evil, and injuries inflicted that are so great, that it seems to us quite impossible that any good can come of them.' Yet this is to reckon without God. And *he* is wholly positive towards man and his self-inflicted hurt. There is no dwelling on guilt, no punishment in love, no wrath in God himself: it is we who cannot but find it hell to live with such a love, which never changes and will never let us go. One feels that she aches for the conclusion that if the love of Calvary is really omnipotent then *all* must eventually be won to it. But she is too loyal a daughter of the medieval church to be the universalist her theology demands.

Here let me concentrate on three things that hit me between the eyes as I read the easy-flowing modern version by Clifton Wolters in the Penguin Classics, from which I quote. In fact they are focussed in fewer than forty pages of it between chapters 51 and 63, none of which, incidentally, are to be found in the shorter extant version. If the material is hers, as surely it is, then it is usually held (as in the latest critical edition of the two texts, *Julian of Norwich, The Showings*, by Edmund Colledge and James Walsh) that she added it later, though this implies that she at first suppressed the parable of the master and his servant which now forms the longest chapter and central vision of the book. For she specifically says that it formed part of the original revelations, even though its full meaning came to her only twenty years later. There seems to me something to be said for the hypothesis that the shorter text, even though our sole surviving manuscript of it is earlier (yet still well after her death), could represent an expurgated edition for popular consumption with the stronger meat and more dangerous thoughts left out! But this, like most else, is a guess.

On the face of it the parable is a simple, not to say simplistic, tale of a medieval lord who is seen

> sitting down quietly, relaxed and peaceful: the servant is standing by his lord, humble and ready to do his bidding. And then I saw the lord look at his servant with rare love and tenderness, and quietly send him to a certain place to fulfil his purpose. Not only

> does that servant go, but he starts off at once, running with all speed, in his love to do what his master wanted. And without warning he falls headlong into a deep ditch, and injures himself very badly.

Clearly, as she says in interpreting her vision, 'The servant stood for Adam, . . . but on the other hand there were many characteristics that could not possibly be ascribed to him.' And here the depths of the parable begin to emerge. As in a play where one actor plays two parts, representing different facets or aspects of the same character, so the servant is not only Adam (who for her even then means not a particular individual but 'All-man' or Everyman) but the Second Person of the Trinity. And she makes the astonishing theological statement that 'When Adam fell, God's Son fell.' 'In all this the good Lord showed his own Son and Adam as one man. . . . Both were shown in the one servant.' This indeed can be dug out of the New Testament itself, where Adam the forebear of Jesus is described in Luke's genealogy as 'son of God' (3.38). What Christ, as God's true son, the authentic Adam, does is to recapitulate everything in the story of man. As in biology 'ontogeny repeats phylogeny', the individual encapsulates the history of the species – spiritually as well as physically. But not only repeats but redeems. As Julian quaintly puts it, 'God's Son fell, with Adam, but into the depths of the Virgin's womb – herself the fairest daughter of Adam.' And he grows up wearing Adam's sweaty and sin-stained clothes. In contrast with patristic and medieval orthodoxy, though not, I believe, with the biblical picture, Christ for her did not take unfallen human nature. Rather, she says, it was

> our filthy, dying flesh which the Son of God took upon himself, like Adam's old coat, tight, threadbare, and too short, [and which] the Saviour transformed into something beautiful, fresh, bright and splendid . . . fairer and richer than even the clothing I had seen on the Father. [The Father's] clothing was blue [the simple colour of the sky], but Christ's was of a harmony and beauty the like and wonder of which I just cannot describe.

All this is strongly reminiscent in our day of the theology of Karl Barth, who at this point was also aware of standing very much against the stream of tradition (though he shows no sign of knowing or acknowledging Julian) in asserting that 'the nature which God took in Christ is identical with our nature under the fall'.

> He was no sinner. But his situation was, both from the inside

> and out, that of a sinner. He freely entered upon solidarity with our lost and wretched state.

Barth too spoke of the Incarnation as 'the journey of the Son of God into a far country' (and we know which son did that journey) and of 'the humanity of God' (rather than the divinity of man).

For Julian the Son of God (with a capital 'S') is no other than *the* true son of God (with a small 's') that we are all created, but fail, to be. If Christ is unique, it is because he alone is normal, the proper man, not because he is abnormal. The *identity* of the two servants, that Adam is the Son of God and *vice versa*, is the mystery of the Incarnation. No wonder it took a long time for what she called 'the inner enlightenment' to dawn, and the implications of it have still to be worked through in our day.

But, secondly, the presuppositions of this understanding of the Incarnation are broader still, and here I think she is sounder than Karl Barth, and closer to the Anglican F. D. Maurice, in arguing for a truly and deeply natural theology. As she put it, 'the Second Person of the Trinity willed to become the foundation and the head of this lovely human nature. From him we come, with him we are included, to him we go.' 'I could see no difference between God and our substance: it was all God, so to speak.' That is not to deny what Kierkegaard called the absolute qualitative difference between the Creator and the creature: 'God is God, and our substance his creation.' But it is to say that 'God is nearer to us than our own soul, for he is the ground in which it stands.' 'I had', she says of her experiences, 'received a touch of God – and it was fundamentally natural.' The supernatural for her is what is superly, supremely natural. For God is 'the substance of everything natural'. And when she says 'everything', she means it – not just the higher spiritual part of man. For 'He is in our sensuality too. The moment our soul was made sensual, at that moment it was destined from all eternity to be the City of God'. 'That wonderful city, the seat of our Lord Jesus Christ, is our sensuality.' Therefore nothing can be regarded as common or unclean:

> The same single love pervades all. . . . In our lower part there are pains and passions, sympathy, pity, mercy and forgiveness, and so on – all most profitable; in the higher part are none of these, but altogether the most tremendous love and marvellous joy.

And in contrast with Eastern and most Western mysticism the

higher part is not bought at the expense of the lower. This is because her theology is so profoundly natural and incarnational. Julian is certainly no nature-mystic, by-passing sin and redemption. It is not, she says, that 'we are going to be saved because God is the foundation of our nature, but only if, from the same source, we receive his mercy and grace'. Yet 'nature and grace are agreed, for both are of God. He works in these two ways, and loves in one.' 'Goodness-by-nature', as she puts it, 'implies God.' And sin is 'really unclean' because it is 'really unnatural'. Her appeal, as in the parables of Jesus, is to the sheer naturalness of grace and to the graciousness of the God of nature who makes his sun to rise on the evil and on the good and is kind to the ungrateful and the selfish. God is so natural, so human, or, as Julian loves to put it, so 'homely'. With Jesus she asks, 'Is there a father among you who will offer his son a stone when he asks for bread, or a snake when he asks for a fish? If you then, bad as you are [and neither of them had any illusions on this], know how to give your children what is good for them, how much more will your heavenly Father!' (Matt. 7.9–11).

But, thirdly, and perhaps most shockingly, she goes on to draw out the likeness of God's love not simply in fatherly but in motherly terms. The comparison of God with a mother caring for her child was already made in the Old Testament (Isa. 49.15; 66.13), and Jesus spoke of himself as a mother hen gathering her chicks (Matt. 23.37; Luke 13.34). Indeed the Epistle of James (1.18) uses the metaphor of God actually giving us birth. Again, there is an underground stream of feminist spirituality in popular medieval piety, including the prayers of Anselm, Archbishop of Canterbury. But the sheer boldness of Julian's language has not been equalled until the women's theology of our day. 'God is as really our Mother as he is our Father.' 'We owe our being to him – and this is the essence of motherhood! – and all the delightful, loving protection which ever follows.'

Above all is this mothering language true of Christ. For in him

> God most high . . . adorned and arrayed himself with our poor flesh, ready to function and serve as Mother in all things. A mother's is the most intimate, willing, and dependable of all services. . . . None has been able to fulfil it properly but Christ, and he alone can. We know that our own mother's bearing of us was a bearing to pain and death, but what does Jesus, our true Mother, do? Why, he . . . carries us within himself in love. And

> he is in labour until the time has fully come for him to suffer the sharpest pangs and most appalling pain possible – and in the end he dies. And not even when this is over, and we ourselves have been born to eternal bliss, is his marvellous love completely satisfied. . . . For he needs to feed us, . . . it is an obligation of his dear, motherly, love. The human mother will suckle her child with her own milk, but our beloved Mother, Jesus, feeds us with himself, and, with the most tender courtesy, does it by means of the Blessed Sacrament. . . . He leads us into his blessed breast through his open side.

Furthermore he continues to bring us up like a human mother, who 'as the child grows older . . . changes her methods – but not her love'. He even 'allows some of us to fall more severely and painfully than ever before'. And we are tempted to think it is all a waste of time.

> It is not so, of course. We need to fall, and we need to realize this. . . . By the simple fact that we fell we shall gain a deep and wonderful knowledge of what God's love means. Love that cannot, will not, be broken by sin, is rock-like, and quite astonishing. It is a good thing to know this. . . . We have *got* to see this.

Finally she clings to the hope that 'every kind of "nature" that he [God] has caused to flow out of himself to fulfil his purpose will be brought back and restored to him', until in the end

> our gracious Mother shall bring us up to our Father's bliss. And then the true meaning of those lovely words will be made known to us, 'It's all going to be all right. You will see yourself that everything is going to be all right.'

It is an astonishingly whole and extraordinarily modern theology. She wants loyally to keep within the answers of the medieval church, but her questions constantly break through them. She claims them as 'revelations of the divine love'. We might equally say that they were intimations welling up from the very depths of her being. But, as she herself says, 'whether our urge is to know God or to know our own soul matters little'. 'God is nearer to us than our own soul, for he is the ground in which it stands.' Indeed, she writes

> I was able to see with absolute certainty that it was easier for us to get to know God than to know our own soul. For our own soul is so deeply set in God. . . . All the same, we can never attain to the full knowledge of God until we have first known

> our own soul thoroughly. Until our soul reaches its full development we can never be completely holy; in other words, *not until our sensuality has been raised to the level of our substance.*

That could have been written by a Tillich or a Jung or a Harry Williams in our day. Knowledge of God, self-awareness and integration of the shadow are all facets of the same thing.

Truly a woman for all seasons. Yet she is this because she is beyond all seasons. The mystic, said Blake, sees 'eternity in a grain of sand'. Julian's image is that of a nut – from which our word 'nuclear' comes.

> And he showed me . . . a little thing, the size of a hazel nut, on the palm of my hand, round like a ball. I looked at it thoughtfully and wondered. 'What is this?' And the answer came, 'It is all that is made.' I marvelled that it continued to exist and did not suddenly disintegrate; it was so small. And again my mind supplied the answer. 'It exists, both now and for ever, because God loves it.' In short everything owes its existence to the love of God.

And 'after this', she says later, 'I saw the whole Godhead concentrated as it were in a single point and thereby I learnt that he is in all things.' But conversely

> Our Lord opened my spiritual eyes, and showed me the soul in the middle of my heart . . . as large as if it were an eternal home, . . . a most glorious city. In the midst of it sat our Lord Jesus Christ, God and man, beautiful in person . . . in rightful peace and rest.

For 'his Godhead rules and upholds both heaven and earth and all that is' – but 'in us *he is completely at home*'.

To make *that* true is indeed the task of eternity.

5. RICHARD JEFFERIES

Who was Richard Jefferies? Despite nearly a hundred entries in the Cambridge University Library catalogue of works by or about him, he remains a stranger to most. He was born, the son of a Wiltshire farmer, in 1848 – yet far removed from the political upheavals that rocked Europe that fateful year. He grew up a dreamy and a solitary genius, with few if any real friends, a lover of the woods, nicknamed Loony Dick or Moony Dick. He became a reporter on the local paper, tried his hand at juvenile novels about London society of which he knew nothing, then one day wrote a letter to *The Times* about the agricultural labourer in Wiltshire. It was a long, long letter of several thousand words which nowadays would never get published at all. But it was a masterly letter, later followed by two others, which made his name among a small but knowledgeable public. He had articles and essays accepted by London magazines on farming and the English countryside, which were subsequently collected in books with titles like *Wild Life in a Southern County* and *The Amateur Poacher*. He had a great gift of evocation, and in introducing the latter book Henry Williamson was later to go so far as to call him 'irregularly the greatest writer in English literature since Shakespeare'. He married a farmer's daughter, and in order to be nearer his publishers went to live near London, at Surbiton. But intestinal tuberculosis, ill-diagnosed and badly treated, forced him to retire to the healthier air first of Brighton and then of Goring, where he died in 1887 after seven years of chronic pain at the age of 38. But during those years his thirsting soul drove him to write and then, when he couldn't, to dictate a great deal more than his frail body could stand – including an autobiography on which he told his publisher that he had been meditating for seventeen years, *The Story of my Heart*. Of this book it could be said, as Walt Whitman said of one of his own, 'This is no book. Who touches this, touches a man.' And it is from it that most of my quotations will be taken.

But first we should never forget that Jefferies was primarily a naturalist, with a quite extraordinarily developed sense of sight. 'He saw things', it has been said, 'as the sun sees them', and he had a rare capacity to transfer this sight to paper. But he was also a seer, a visionary, able to see in things and beyond things to a world that for him streamed through them with palpable, almost painful, intensity.

At first sight he appears to be a typical nature-mystic with a strong sense of the immanence of the spiritual in the natural:

> Through every glass-blade in the thousand, thousand grasses; through the million leaves, veined and edge-cut, on bush and tree; through the song-notes and the marked feathers of the birds; through the insects' hum and the colour of the butterflies; through the soft warm air, the flecks of clouds dissolving – I used them all for prayer.

He has an exquisite, almost excruciating, sense of the presence of what he called 'the Beyond' pressing and pulsing through earth, sky, sea, and above all through the rays of the sun.

Yet there are two things that should be noticed about Jefferies' nature-mysticism. He is no romantic townsman seeking escape in the unspoilt countryside. Some of his most mystical and poignant passages are set in the heart and throb of London itself. Leaning over the parapet of London Bridge, he writes,

> I felt the presence of the immense powers of the universe; I felt out into the depths of the ether. So intensely conscious of the sun, the sky, the limitless space, I felt too in the midst of eternity then, in the midst of the supernatural, among the immortal, and the greatness of the material realized the spirit. By these I saw my soul; by these I knew the supernatural to be more intensely real than the sun. I touched the supernatural, the immortal, there that moment.

And there is a vivid description of the scene outside the Royal Exchange as the seething surge of men, women and traffic converge, jostle and part, agitated by the 'friction of a thousand interests' and 'beaten like seaweed against the solid walls of fact'. What will be the sum and outcome, Jefferies reflects, of all this ceaseless labour and movement, the jingle and jangle of this unresolvable noise, a hundred years from now? We could revisit the scene today, with little to add to his description but the fumes of fossil-fuels equally doomed to exhaustion, and ponder the same question.

For the other thing about Jefferies' nature-mysticism is that it is entirely unsentimental. There is, he recognizes, 'nothing human in nature', nothing that cares a jot for personal values. Indeed it is anti-human. Nor is there any god in nature, nor any evidence that he can see of mind or design or benevolent purpose. In fact, if the cruelty and the 'immense misery of man' were *meant* there would be no hope of improvement. Like the Preacher of Ecclesiastes, he is forced to the conclusion that 'time and chance happen to all'. In this sense he is as sceptical as any nineteenth-century atheist.

But he refuses to leave it there. And two things will not let him rest. The first is his insatiable thirst, in what he called the 'moral drought' of the world in which we are forced to live, for the unrealized potential of human life, physical and spiritual. He has a biting piece of social criticism, describing the suppressed animosity, the concentrated hatred, of the sullen poor, to which the complacent charity of the well-to-do is blissfully insensitive. As an analysis of the coiled springs of communal violence and mindless vandalism, of wife-beating and explosives sent through the post, it can still send a shudder down the spine. The way in which the poor, the imbecile and the elderly were treated was for him but part of the terrible contradiction and denial – as was his own racked and wasted frame – of what men might be, if delivered from the chain of want and disease and the treadmill of labour. Bodily perfection and the beauty of the flesh cried out to be matched by the enlargement of soul-life to which the 'open-handed generosity' and 'divine waste' of nature beckoned. Like other Victorian visionaries, and Blake before them, Jefferies burned with a passion for a different future for the human race, even for one in which physical death would be transcended. Yet he put no trust like many of them in science (the naturalist's observation, 'the ever watching eye', for him yielded far more than contrived experiment) or progress or even evolution, a 'modern superstition', as he called it, which he vigorously denied. He had the strengths and weaknesses of the self-educated man and isolated genius. Yet one has a hunch that his hour may be at hand, to judge by such recent writings as *The Vision of Glory* by John Stewart Collis, described, as he might have been, as 'the poet among the ecologists', or even by the seeming science-fiction of books like *Supernature* and *The Secret Life of Plants*. For the dogmatism and materialism of Victorian science, which he said 'shut out the soul', are yielding as surely as are the confines of Victorian religion and theism against which Jefferies also bruised his battered spirit.

And this brings me to the second thing that would not let him rest.

I have said that he was an atheist. Yet his was no reductionist or cynical atheism. It was a passionate and positive protest. The traditional idea of God as an omnipotent being to whom to address petitions or as a directing intelligence manipulating nature and history – this man-made figure seemed to him (as later to Bonhoeffer) blasphemously inadequate to the reality which the soul touches but cannot hope to grasp. He regarded it as 'an invisible idol'. 'The mind goes on and requires more. . ., something higher than deity.' And he links this with the need to press beyond the 'three ideas' of man's inner consciousness which in the course of civilization have so far been 'wrested from the unknown' – 'the existence of the soul, immortality and deity'. These concepts are but projections by which humanity's intimations of the Beyond are given objective and substantial shape. Jefferies had no desire to go back on them. They are pointers, 'stepping stones' to a 'fourth idea', or rather to an illimitable series of ideas, 'an immense ocean over which the mind can sail, upon which the vessel of thought has not yet been launched'.

> The mind of so many thousand years has worked round and round inside the circle of these three ideas as a boat on an inland lake. Let us haul it over the belt of land, launch it on the ocean, and sail outwards.

The God of nineteenth-century theism was for Jefferies just too small. He *had* to be denied and transcended. 'By the Beyond', he wrote in the notebooks of his last pain-racked years, 'I mean the Idea of the *whole*: that would fill the sky.' It is the same vision as that of the thirteenth-century Umbrian mystic, Angela of Foligno, who influenced Teilhard de Chardin, a visionary of nature not unlike Jefferies, except of course that he gladly embraced both science and evolution. She said this:

> The eyes of my soul were opened and I beheld the plenitude of God, wherein I did comprehend the whole world, both here and beyond the sea, the abyss and the ocean and all things. In all these things I beheld naught save the divine power, in a manner assuredly inscrutable; so that through excess of marvelling the soul cried with a loud voice, saying: 'The whole world is full of God.'

Jefferies would not have put it that way. Yet without using God-language he wrote:

> I was not more than eighteen when an inner and esoteric meaning began to come to me from all this visible universe, and indefinable aspirations filled me. . . . There was a deeper meaning everythwere. . . . I was sensitive to all things, to the earth under, and the star-hollow round about; to the least blade of grass, to the largest oak. They seemed like exterior nerves and veins for the conveyance of feeling to me. Sometimes a very ecstasy of exquisite enjoyment of the entire visible universe filled me.

Finally, here are some words of a man who was condemned in his time as an atheist and who, though he spoke with pathos of 'the voice that ceased on the cross', felt compelled to say, 'I am a pagan' because 'I think the heart and soul above crowns':

> At the mouth of the ancient cave, face to face with the unknown, the cavemen prayed. Prone in heart today I pray, Give me the

> deepest soul-life. . . . Not tomorrow but today. . . . Now is eternity, now I am in the midst of immortality; now the supernatural crowds around me. Open my mind, give my soul to see, let me live it now on earth.

Whether on his deathbed, as his first biographer said, 'the simple old faith came back to him' and he died a Christian is unproven and indeed improbable. He remains a man of the fields and a free-thinker. What he called the 'immensity' of his 'prayer-desire' is not to be cabined or confined.

So let us leave him in his open air, with a passage that catches something of his style as well as his spirit:

> There were grass-grown tumuli on the hills to which of old I used to walk, sit down at the foot of one of them, and think. Some warrior had been interred there in the ante-historic times. The sun of the summer mornings shone on the dome of the sward, and the air came softly up from the wheat below, the tips of the grasses swayed as it passed sighing faintly, it ceased, and the bees hummed by to the thyme and the heathbells. I became absorbed in the glory of the day, the sunshine, the sweet air, the yellowing corn turning from its sappy green to the summer's noon of gold, the lark's song like a waterfall in the sky. I felt at that moment that I was like the spirit of the man whose body was interred in the tumulus; I could understand and feel his existence the same as my own. . . .
>
> Look at another person while living; the soul is not visible, only the body which it animates. Therefore, merely because after death the soul is not visible is no demonstration that it does not still live. The condition of being unseen is the same condition which occurs while the body is living, so that intrinsically there is nothing exceptionable, or supernatural, in the life of the soul after death. . . . Only by the strongest effort of the mind could I understand the idea of extinction; that was supernatural, requiring a miracle; the immortality of the soul natural, like earth. Listening to the sighing of the grass I felt immortality as I felt the beauty of the summer morning, and I thought beyond immortality, of other conditions, more beautiful than existence, higher than immortality.

Like Julian of Norwich, of whom he would certainly never have heard, Richard Jefferies believed passionately in the utter naturalness of the Beyond. And like the spirit of the man in the tumulus of whom he wrote that 'it was to me really alive, and very close', surely he too, being dead, yet speaks.

6. JOSEPH BARBER LIGHTFOOT

There could scarcely have been a greater contrast than that between Richard Jefferies and Joseph Barber Lightfoot, even though they were contemporaries. Lightfoot was born twenty years earlier than Jefferies, in 1828, and died two years later, in 1889. Jefferies was a loner, a self-taught man, a lover of the fields and flowers, frail in physique, a sceptic and a mystic. Lightfoot, though described as a man of 'imperturbable silence', was always surrounded by colleagues and students, a product of the best classical education of his or perhaps any age, a man of books and a burner of the midnight oil, a figure of powerful build, a firm believer and an efficient organizer. (A friend once said of Lightfoot that he ought to have been 'the chairman of an English Railway Company – and I wish I had shares in it!') Yet both are leaves of the same tree of life, rooted in the same English soil, and I find that each speaks strongly to different parts of myself.

Unlike Jefferies, Lightfoot will always be remembered as one of a trio, Lightfoot, Westcott and Hort, who together a hundred years ago made English, and indeed Cambridge, and indeed Trinity, New Testament scholarship a wonder of the world. My father had the fortune to be an undergraduate at Cambridge at the time and I have his manuscript notes on 'St Paul's Epistle to the Romans by Professor Lightfoot, October term 1876', and the year before he had heard Hort on Romans, Westcott on St John and Lightfoot on I Corinthians. There was a single *annus mirabilis* in 1878–9, before Lightfoot moved to be Bishop of Durham, when all three held theological chairs there together, Lightfoot the Lady Margaret, Hort the Hulsean, and Westcott the Regius – for which last Lightfoot (the youngest of the three) had refused to stand in 1870 so that Westcott, his senior at Trinity and successor at Durham, could return to Cambridge to hold it.

Lightfoot had himself first been appointed to the Hulsean chair in 1861 at the age of 33 – and it is some consolation to the rest of us to learn that he actually failed to get it the year before! In fact the man appointed, who happily became a bishop within a year, so dismayed Lightfoot, who had earlier shown up the inadequacy of his scholarship (as he was later to do so devastatingly with the unfortunate author of *Supernatural Religion*, who under the cloak of anonymity had dared question Westcott's scholarly integrity) that he resolved that night to give up theological studies and return to the classics!

The date 1861 is significant. For the 1860s were to prove as turbulent a decade in English church history as the 1960s. They were to see the publication of the symposium *Essays and Reviews*, the battle between Thomas Huxley and Bishop Wilberforce on the Darwinian controversy, and the crisis over biblical criticism sparked by Colenso's writings on the Pentateuch. Yet still another event had left its aftermath with which it fell to Lightfoot in particular to deal.

1860 saw the death of Ferdinand Christian Baur, Professor of Church History and Dogmatics at Tübingen. He had dominated the scene of German scholarship for a generation and as a result of his work the foundations of New Testament study had been turned upside down. Very little of the traditional edifice remained intact. Only five of its books were by apostles or came from apostolic times – Romans, I and II Corinthians and Galatians by Paul and Revelation by John, dating from the 50s and the late 60s respectively. The rest were composed up to and beyond the middle of the second century AD to patch up what Baur saw as the all-consuming conflict in the early church between the narrow Jewish Christianity of Jesus' original disciples, represented by Peter and John, and the universalistic message proclaimed by Paul. The fact that the gospels and others books of the New Testament were cited by church Fathers towards the end of the second century alone set an upper limit to their dating. Their historicity, especially that of the Fourth Gospel, which was dated between 160 and 170, was minimal. Other writers went still further than Baur and declared every one of the New Testament books to be pseudonymous.

Lightfoot's achievement, written up by Bishop Stephen Neill, himself a Fellow of Trinity, in his *Interpretation of the New Testament, 1861 – 1961*, was to expose the flimsiness of the historical foundations of this whole construction. For Lightfoot was primarily the historian of the trio, with Westcott the theologian and social reformer and Hort the wider thinker and natural scientist – though as the Westcott and Hort text of the Greek Testament reminds us, each by modern standards was equipped in almost every field. And Lightfoot did this task not primarily by the work on the New Testament for which he is now most remembered, but, as he himself put it, by ' "repairing a breach" not indeed in the House of the Lord itself, but in the immediately outlying buildings'. This was in his massive work on the Apostolic Fathers, particularly Clement of Rome, Ignatius and Polycarp, which occupied him for the best part of thirty years, and on which he was still working as he dropped unconscious three days before his death. By rigorous historical investigation he established the authenticity of the first Epistle of Clement, which he dated at 95–6, and of seven genuine Epistles of Ignatius, between 110 and 115. In each of these authors both Peter and Paul are celebrated in the same breath without a trace of rivalry and he showed once and for all how groundless were Baur's second-century datings for New Testament writings that must have preceded them. This achievement was acknowledged by the great German scholar Adolf von Harnack who, while often on the other side of the scholarly argument, wrote of him: 'There has never been an apologist who was less of an advocate than Lightfoot. . . . He has never defended a tradition for the tradition's sake.' In everything he touched he was scrupulously fair both to the evidence and to his opponents; and, as his friend Dean Farrar noted of him, he was virtually unique as a controversialist who made no enemies and attracted no abuse. The Oxford scholar, William Sanday, in an encomium which must have embarrassed Lightfoot in his lifetime, confessed that neither Oxford nor Germany could match him for what he went on to detail as: exactness of scholarship, width of erudition, scientific method, sobriety of judgment and lucidity of style. In all these he was massive and magisterial. Indeed, as I found when working on my own *Redating the New Testament*, Lightfoot is the one of the three who still scarcely dates. One may dare to dissent from his conclusions; but only at one minor point have I caught Homer nodding, and once, but only once, C. H. Dodd actually accused him of making an irresponsible conjecture! His commentaries on the Epistles of St Paul set a new model and have never been surpassed, and his little known lectures on 'The Authenticity of St John's Gospel', published posthumously in his *Biblical Essays*, anticipated and in my judgment have outlasted the work of Westcott to whom he deferred.

In the course of preparing this I feel I have lived with a giant. I think I have read virtually everything that has been written about him – and a handful of dust it is. For he has never had a proper biography, only a collection of tributes edited by G. R. Eden and F. C. Macdonald, entitled *Lightfoot of Durham*. His dying friend Hort did the entry in the *Dictionary of National Biography*, and more recently C. K. Barrett gave a most accomplished paper on him to the

Durham University Lightfoot Society, which was published in *The Durham University Journal* for June 1972.

Yet through each of the fragmentary memoirs, of which that in A. C. Benson's *Leaves of the Tree* is much the most vivid, there meets us a man who bestrode his generation like a colossus. Deeply rooted in a knowledge of Greek and Latin, as well as Hebrew, Syriac, Arabic, Ethiopic, Coptic and Armenian, he was also so freely at home in modern languages that he once remarked in all innocence to an astonished chaplain, 'Does it not sometimes happen to you that when you have read a book you forget in what language it is written?' To another former pupil and domestic chaplain, my uncle Armitage Robinson, he sent notes while Bishop of Durham requesting him to verify obscure references which reveal the astonishing range of his learning and his relentless attention to precision of detail. He was a man of prodigious industry and elephantine memory (and ugliness!). During his time at Trinity, where he occupied Newton's old rooms, it was said of him by H. C. G. Moule, his pupil and successor but one at Durham, 'No man ever loitered so late in the Great Court that he did not see Lightfoot's lamp burning in his study window, though no man either was so regularly present in morning Chapel at seven o'clock that he did not find Lightfoot always there with him.' He was also active in University affairs and in founding the Theological Tripos. He was a member of the Council of the Senate for sixteen years and a pamphlet survives from 1877 opposing a grace for abolishing compulsory attendance at professors' lectures – not that *he* required any such sanctions! The great dining hall at Trinity was the only room big enough for his courses on the Greek New Testament.

For much of this time also he was heavily committed to work on the Revised Version (for which, unhappily, he defended the rule that the same word in the same contexts should always be rendered by the same word in English), and he did regular preaching residence as a Canon of St Paul's. At Durham too, to which he gave himself unsparingly, he continued to fit in his academic writing before breakfast or late at night, and could be seen correcting proofs in the stern of a boat on his summer holidays. But it was too much even for his constitution and at the relatively early age of 61 he died, symbolically, of an enlarged heart. For he was a big man in every way, except in height (I have tried on his episcopal ring, which was as vast as his spectacles were minute!). He inspired enormous personal devotion in those among whom he laboured in the industrial north; and as his funeral cortège moved from Durham to Auckland Castle, wrote Hort, 'almost every shop was shut and blind down'. This devotion was particularly marked among those 'sons', as he called them, whom he trained for the priesthood in his own house and (like so much else, including a large stained glass window in Trinity Chapel and a whole church in Sunderland) at his own expense. My uncle wrote of his generation growing up under the shadow of Lightfoot, Westcott and Hort: 'We never ceased to be conscious of how inferior was the breed of the "Epigoni", inferior in intellectual vigour and in power of concentration, but inferior above all in that intensity of moral and religious conviction which makes the worker so much greater than his work.'

As another was to say of Lightfoot at his death, 'If he has not done all he intended, he has at least shown how it should be done. He has left the legacy of an ideal greater than the actual which he made so great.' Though he wrote vastly more than Hort, he was conscious of how much more remained to be done, including a history of the church in the fourth century for which his notable article on Eusebius of Caesarea in the *Dictionary of Christian Biography* was an early study. Above all his commentaries on the Pauline Epistles, apart from notes published posthumously, were sadly unfinished. What Armitage called the 'well-meant if not well-chosen words' of an illuminated address of welcome presented to him at Auckland Castle that 'many more Epistles of St Paul might flow from his Lordship's pen' remained a pious wish.

But in the last resort what he showed us is *how* to contend for the truth. Faced with the challenges of the 1860s and 1870s, many distrusted scholarship, feared biblical criticism and sought to settle questions of history with the answers of dogma. Lightfoot and his friends saw that the only valid response was sounder scholarship, better history and a more critical faith. The church owes them an inestimable debt. Today there are again plenty who would meet the attacks of our age with relapse into fundamentalisms of various kinds. Ports like this may seem safe in a storm, but if the church of a hundred years ago had not had the courage and the scholarship to launch out into the deep, it would be impossible today to be both a scientist and a Christian. For that task we need to be equipped with what St Paul calls the 'panoply', the whole armour, of God (Eph. 6.13). We have not all got it and none of us has got it all, and the bits most of us have are largely second-hand. But when a champion appears in the field we should rally to him and look up. It was he who said that 'history is the best cordial for drooping spirits'. His example, in our midst and so nearly in our own time, should surely nerve us, as St Paul goes on, 'to withstand in the evil day, and having done all to stand'.

Lightfoot's self-chosen task was to defend the historical base of the Christian gospel, and in fresh forms that remains a perennial task. But the method he used and the rigour and integrity with which he taught us to pursue it have constantly to be applied on other and wider fronts and in ever-changing areas. Only recently a book has appeared in English whose title well catches, I think, the spirit in which Lightfoot lived: *On Having a Critical Faith*. It is the translation of a short work by a German New Testament scholar, Gerd Theissen, which he says has meant more to him than any of his professional studies. It goes back, he tells us, to his student days and his dissatisfaction with the attitude of so many of his theological teachers. How could they go on working, day after day, when they could not even give a convincing answer to the charge that God is an illusion. 'I resolved either to find an answer of my own or give up theology altogether.'

The details of this exercise do not concern us here and they are naturally conditioned by the current German debate. But it is an exercise that has to be undertaken afresh in every culture and every generation. Indeed it is something that we each of us have to do for ourselves over a lifetime – facing faith at every point, with the question, 'Is it true?' That is a question that can surprisingly easily be evaded or glossed over. Writing nearly twenty years ago now in *The Honest to God Debate*, David Edwards noted the various movements for renewal in the church which then and since have evoked hope and enthusiasm, and he said: 'But they all share one defect: *they do not necessarily concern the truth of Christianity*', and he added: 'A deeper renewal is needed which may involve a costlier change.'

Professor Theissen closes his book with these words:

> I am not interested in irrefutable assertions but in refutable truths. This question of truth goes against much in life that is otherwise valuable. It causes resentment, at a time when agreement with others counts more than the corrections of the errors of yesterday and today. It is not legitimated by faithfulness to the tradition, but shows its faithfulness to the tradition by being open to cross-examination. But it is open to argument, even to argument from dogmatic traditions. It allows itself to be irritated by arguments, for it is based on the recognition 'that I may be wrong and you may be right, and by an effort we may get nearer to the truth.'

That last sentence is a quotation from Karl Popper, whose influence can be recognized behind the words 'I am not interested in irrefutable assertions but in refutable truths'. For his great contribution has been to insist that statements can be scientific only if they are falsifiable. If nothing can be brought against a theory that could refute it, then it cannot be true.

Lightfoot would have liked that. He believed in hard evidence (Lightfoot's mental interests, wrote Hort to Westcott, 'lay almost exclusively in concrete facts or written words'), and he marshalled it with massive expertise and scrupulous fairness. 'Great is truth and it shall prevail' was a conviction by which he lived, and, though most do not realize it, that comes not from classical humanism but from scripture (I Esd. 4.35). And for the Christian, as Hort insisted in his famous Hulsean Lectures, *The Way, the Truth, the Life*, Christ is the truth. Every truth therefore, as Westcott loved to stress, whether it comes from science or art or history or other religions, must eventually lead to him rather than away from him. Such is the deep trust of a genuinely critical faith, which

> . . . makes the children free
> To follow truth and *thus* to follow thee.

This freedom is the opposite of the spirit of fear with which, for instance, the legally minded Tertullian operated. As Elaine Pagels says, in her recent book *The Gnostic Gospels*,

> He complains that they [the Gnostics] refused simply to accept and believe the rule of faith as others did: instead, they challenged others to raise theological questions, when they themselves claimed no answers, being ready to say, and sincerely, of certain points of their belief, 'This is not so', and 'I take this in a different sense', and 'I do not admit to that.' Tertullian warns that such questioning leads to heresy.

That is the fear of an *un*critical faith – that even to raise questions 'makes men heretics'. The Gnostics (whose detachment of the faith from history Lightfoot would have stood wholly with Irenaeus in condemning) we now know accused the orthodox, as Ivan Karamazov was to do later, of seducing men and women from 'the truth of their freedom'. That phrase, with its corollary 'the freedom of their truth', perhaps sums up as well as any the ground for which the Cambridge triumvirate contended. And of the three, the greatest, or rather the *primus inter pares*, remains for me Joseph Barber Lightfoot.

POSTSCRIPT

Reviewing the concerns that these chapters have reflected I have become convicted that there is one which I have almost irresponsibly left unaddressed. It looms so large, it seems so immeasurably beyond the power of any individual to affect, that we get used to doing our theology like our living as if it were hardly there. I have referred to it, but only peripherally. Yet the chances of any of us still being alive in 1990 to reflect on the *next* ten years must depend upon our coming to terms with it. And at the time of writing these chances must realistically be assessed at a good deal less than even. Never, even at the time of the Berlin air-lift or the Cuba missiles-crisis, has the world stood closer to the brink of destruction by nuclear holocaust. Yet the current calls are for stepping up rather than stopping the arms race. The priorities alike of the present or foreseeable British, American and Soviet administrations are, at a time of deepening recession, for ever-mounting military expenditure, and the drift into accidental annihilation becomes increasingly alarming. In one week while I was recently in the United States there were two false alerts in the missile defence system, thanks to a defective computer now 'retired'!

An image from that visit has remained vividly in my mind. Lying in bed in Los Angeles on a Saturday night I heard the familiar ferocious screeching of brakes, followed by what seemed the long seconds' delay before the sickening shattering thud. Then the sirens of the police, then of the ambulance. At least one instinctively assumes that was the sequence: for in our society security is quicker on the draw than succour. It was an only too usual part of a scene which accepts 60,000 road deaths a year as though they were an act of God. Indeed there appeared to be almost no household I met that week who had not had someone affected – starting with the university chaplain who drove me from the airport, who had just adopted the sole surviving daughter of his brother's entire family, obliterated in a single crash. But it struck me that moment as symbolic also of a still more horrifying collision-course, which one immediately senses as heightened, like most other things, on arrival in the USA. In its aftermath there will be neither ambulances nor even police, and the dead will be the fortunate ones. Meanwhile one has the same sense of helpless impotence, asking with George Kennan, the former US Ambassador to Moscow, 'Must it be this way? Can it be true that we can do no better than this? Can it really be that we have no choice but to march blindly forward, like lemmings, into a sea of hopeless catastrophe?'

From the other side of the gulf André Sakharov, the banished Russian dissident, has said unequivocally: 'I believe that the problem of lessening the danger of the annihilation of humanity in a nuclear war carries absolute priority over all other considerations.' For if this issue is not resolved there will be no others to resolve. Indeed it might seem that beside it all others pale into insignificance, so that most of the concerns of this book come to look irrelevant luxuries. On the contrary I believe they are sharpened and made the more urgent by it.

That same week the *Los Angeles Times* ran an article showing how responsible energy conservation could save every barrel of oil the US needs to import from the Middle East. Relieved of that dependence and vulnerability the world would be an infinitely safer place. Again, the export for commercial gain of nuclear power plants, unsafe even at home, has so obvious a connection with world instability and planetary pollution as to need no further underlining. Only less slightly blatantly the problems of urban violence and racial disaffection, of mass unemployment and poverty, are a direct result of sinful mismanagement of the earth's resources. It was General Eisenhower, no pacifist, who said: 'Every gun made, every warship launched, every rocket fired, signifies a theft from those who hunger, and are not fed; those who are cold, and are not clothed.' But behind these more immediately palpable connections every loss in liberality, every erosion of critical faith, strengthens the conformity to this world on which the political consensus rests that makes the whole mad process seem irresistible.

Not only does it mesmerize the voter, but it gags the church in a way that must surely seem unbelievable to our successors – if we have any. Whereas now on *apartheid* the main-line leadership of the church is ready to risk arrest and imprisonment, on the issues of war, despite successively stronger Lambeth Conference resolutions, it is largely left to those who can be written off as pacifists or lefties, unilateralists or 'wets'. All honour to them – whether one agrees with their political analyses or not. But governments will not listen until there is a massive passive resistance – say, on the refusal to pay the tax-proportion required for the arms race – from both leaders and led who cannot be so dismissed. The momentum that still has to be built up is daunting. In the words of one who is fighting courageously from within the Episcopal Church of the United States, George F. Regas, the Rector of All Saints', Pasadena: 'People easily accuse the peacemaker of being soft-headed and impracticable. Reversing the arms race in today's political climate is politically unacceptable. However, policies leading to extinction of the human race seem to be accepted as thoroughly sound politically. That borders on madness.'

Within the next few years I believe we have got to see a profound change of heart and direction, involving East and West, North and South alike, if all our futures, like our yesterdays, are not to lead the way to dusty death. Who is capable of such things? None of us in our own powers or imaginations. Yet here is something surely on which the voices of all Christians from the first, second and third worlds, not to mention those of other faiths, must be able to unite – and if they cannot on this then they deserve to perish from the earth. Yet for this enormous resources of spirituality will be demanded, requiring deep dedication both to the centre and to the edges – and a supply of men and women more rooted and more radical than anything that recent decades have had to show.

August 1980 *John Robinson*

BOOK LIST

Dates and publishers of the more recent books mentioned in the text.

Altizer, T., *The Gospel of Christian Atheism*, Westminster Press 1966, Collins 1967

Alves, R., *A Theology of Human Hope*, World Publishing Co. 1969; A. Clarke 1975

American Catholic Exodus, ed. J. O'Connor, Corpus Books, Washington DC 1969

Bonhoeffer, D., *Christology*, Eng. trs., Fontana Books 1971
Carter, S., *Love More or Less*, Galliard 1971
Christian Believing, Doctrine Commission of the Church of England, SPCK 1976
Collis, J. S., *The Vision of Glory* (1972), Penguin Books 1975
Davis, C., *Body as Spirit*, Hodder & Stoughton 1977
Davis, W., *It's No Sin to be Rich*, Osprey, London 1976
Devlin, Lord, *The Enforcement of Morals*, Oxford University Press 1965
Dillistone, F. W., *C. H. Dodd*, Hodder & Stoughton 1977
Dumitriu, P., *Incognito*, Eng. trs., Collins and Macmillan, New York, 1964
Edwards, D. L., ed., *The Honest to God Debate*, SCM Press and Westminster Press 1963
Facing Up to Nuclear Power, ed. J. Francis and P. Abrecht, St Andrew Press 1976
Garrison, J., *From Hiroshima to Harrisburg*, SCM Press 1980
Geering, L., *Faith's New Age*, Collins, 1980
Goulder, M., ed., *Incarnation and Myth: The Debate Continued*, SCM Press and Eerdmans 1978
Green, M., ed., *The Truth of God Incarnate*, Hodder & Stoughton 1977
Grollenberg, L., *Palestine Comes First*, SCM Press 1980
Haley, A., *Roots*, Doubleday 1976; Hutchinson 1977
Hammarskjøld, D., *Markings*, Knopf and Faber & Faber 1964
Hart, H. L. A., *Law, Liberty and Morality*, Oxford University Press 1968
Haughton, R., *On Trying to be Human*, Geoffrey Chapman and Templegate, Springfield, Ill., 1966
The Transformation of Man, Geoffrey Chapman and Templegate 1967
Hebblethwaite, P., *The New Inquisition?*, Fount Books 1980
Hick, J., ed., *The Myth of God Incarnate*, SCM Press and Westminster Press 1977
Jennings, P., ed., *Face to Face with the Turin Shroud*, Mayhew-McCrimmon and Mowbray 1978
Julian of Norwich, *Revelations of Divine Love*, ed. C. Wolters, Penguin Books 1973
The Showings, ed. E. Colledge and J. Walsh, SPCK 1979
Jung, C. G., *Answer to Job* (Coll. Works, Vol. 11, 1958), Routledge & Kegan Paul 1979
Klostermaier, K., *Hindu and Christian in Vrindaban*, Eng. trs. SCM Press 1969
Knox, J., The Limits of Unbelief, Collins and Seabury Press 1970
The Humanity and Divinity of Christ, Cambridge University Press 1967
Never Far from Home, Word Books, Waco, Texas, 1974
Kroll, U., *Lament for a Lost Enemy*, SPCK 1977
Lampe, G. W. H., *God as Spirit*, Oxford University Press 1977
Levin, B., *The Pendulum Years*, Cape (= *Run It Down the Flagpole*, Atheneum Publishers), 1970
Mackey, J. P., *Jesus: The Man and the Myth*, SCM Press and Paulist Press 1979
Moltmann, J., *The Theology of Hope*, Eng. trs., SCM Press and Harper & Row 1967

Neill, S., *The Interpretation of the New Testament 1861–1961*, Oxford University Press 1966
Newsome, D., *The Parting of Friends: A Study of the Wilberforces and Henry Manning*, John Murray and Harvard University Press 1966
Norman, E., *Christianity and World Order*, Oxford University Press 1979
Page, R. J., *New Directions in Anglican Theology: from Temple to Robinson*, Allenson 1965
Pagels, E., *The Gnostic Gospels*, Random House, 1979; Weidenfeld and Nicholson 1980
Panikkar, R., *Intra-Religious Dialogue*, Paulist Press 1978
Phillips, J. B., *Your God is Too Small*, Epworth Press 1952
Pike, J. A., *A Time for Christian Candor*, Harper & Row 1964; Hodder & Stoughton 1965
Pittenger, N., *The Word Incarnate*, Nisbet 1944
Ramsey, A. M., *From Gore to Temple*, Longmans (= *Era in Anglican Theology*, Scribners) 1960
Ramsey, P., *Basic Christian Ethics*, Scribners 1950; SCM Press 1953
Robinson, J. A. T., *The Body* (1952), 9th impression, SCM Press and Westminster Press 1977
On Being the Church in the World, SCM Press 1960; Westminster Press 1962; reissued Mowbrays 1977
Honest to God, SCM Press and Westminster Press 1963
Christian Morals Today, SCM Press 1964
The Human Face of God, SCM Press and Westminster Press 1973
Redating the New Testament, SCM Press and Westminster Press 1976
Can We Trust the New Testament?, Mowbray and Eerdmans 1977
Truth is Two-Eyed, SCM Press and Westminster Press 1979
Schoonenberg, P., *The Christ*, Eng. trs., Herder & Herder and Sheed & Ward 1972
Spicer, F., *Sex and the Love Relationship*, Priory Press, London 1972
Sykes, S., *The Integrity of Anglicanism*, Mowbray 1978
Temple, W., *Christianity and the Social Order* (1942), reissued SPCK 1976
Theissen, G., *On Having a Critical Faith*, Eng. trs., SCM Press and Fortress Press 1979
Thornton, L., *The Common Life in the Body of Christ*, Dacre Press 1963
Tompkins, Peter, *The Secret Life of Plants*, Avon Books, 1974; Penguin Books 1975
Van Buren, P., *The Secular Meaning of the Gospel*, Macmillan, New York, and SCM Press 1963
Watson, Lyall, *Supernature*, Doubleday and Hodder & Stoughton 1973
Vidler, A., ed., *Soundings*, Cambridge University Press 1962
White, P., *The Solid Mandala*, Penguin Books 1974

INDEX OF NAMES